SOCCER
WORLD CUP
2010
PREVIEW

This is a Sevenoaks book.

This edition was published in 2010

A CIP catalogue record for this book is available from the
British Library

10 9 8 7 6 5 4 3 2 1

ISBN: 978-1-84732-563-1

Printed in Hong Kong

SOCCER
WORLD CUP
2010
PREVIEW

SEVENOAKS

CONTENTS

INTRODUCTION

The 2010 soccer World Cup brings the world's greatest entertainment to a brand new stage when Africa becomes a new host continent. South Africa welcomes the soccer world for the greatest single-sport extravaganza on the planet.

The United States is among the 31 national teams which have qualified for the 19th finals in the history of the World Cup. This is the Americans' sixth successive appearance in the finals. That proud record is bettered by only Argentina, Brazil, Germany, Italy, South Korea, and Spain.

Coach Bob Bradley's men march into soccer history and in a setting of which they learned plenty at the Confederations Cup last June. The US competed as reigning champions of Central and North America and did CONCACAF proud by finishing runners-up to Brazil.

It could have been even better. After 27 minutes of the final in Ellis Park, Johannesburg, the US led 2-0. Brazil then hit back in the style and manner of potential World Cup winners to win 3-2 and hand out early warning of their ambition to secure a record-extending sixth triumph.

America's new generation go to South Africa with a mission after being first-round failures in the last finals in Germany in 2006. That was particularly disappointing after the promise of a quarter-finals appearance in Japan and Korea in 2002. Now a record take-up of ticket-buying travelers to South Africa and fans watching from their couches back in the US of A will see Bradley and his men start over.

They do so against a context of remarkable modern-day history in a country which has made giant strides since the historic day 20 years ago when Nelson Mandela walked out of the Victor Verster prison.

Having launched the Rainbow Nation down the irreversible road to unification, Mandela then defied doctors' orders to travel to Zurich in 2004 when FIFA's executive committee awarded the finals to South Africa.

Not only could the bidding triumph not have been achieved without him, it could not even have been undertaken without him. Only in 1992 had South Africa been welcomed back into the FIFA family after the segregationist policy of apartheid had taken the country out into the sporting cold.

Now South Africa, a fascinating and unique country whose people have a passion and a pride in soccer which is equaled in few other nations, is preparing to welcome the world.

Soccer has been played in what is now South Africa since the late 19th century and has always been the sport of the majority black population, even if the rest of the world remained for too long in ignorance of the fact.

Bafana Bafana went beyond even their own fans dreams by reaching the semi-finals of the Confederations Cup, the eight-nation warm-up event staged in June of 2009. "The Boys" even threatened to beat European champions Spain before losing narrowly in the third place play-off.

Match ticket application for the Finals were massively over-subscribed by fans from all around the world who have been happily prepared to make whatever financial sacrifices have been necessary to beat the worldwide recession. They all knew they will be privileged witnesses to a unique event in the history of world sport – and in a country whose historical, cultural and tourist opportunities are like no other.

South Africa will welcome the world with a song and dance and the unique chorus of the vuvuzela horns which invest the land's football with an atmosphere like that at no other World Cup.

United States' DaMarcus Beasley (7) celebrates with teammates Heath Pearce (15), Brian Ching (11), and Landon Donovan (10) after scoring against Cuba in qualifying.

TEAM USA'S MARCH TO THE FINALS

The United States' long journey to South Africa began with an 8-0 win over Barbados in Los Angeles on June 15, 2008. It ended in the fifth minute of stoppage time with a dramatic 2-2 draw against Costa Rica in Washington on October 14, 2009.

Defender Jonathan Bornstein's late, late equaliser preserved the US' unbeaten home record throughout the qualifiers and condemned Costa Rica to an unsuccessful play-off against South American hopefuls Uruguay.

Team USA had already qualified but they fought back from 2-0 down after 23 minutes to top the final CONCACAF group, a point ahead of old rivals Mexico.

They had suffered a major blow in the build-up when striker Charlie Davies was seriously hurt in a car crash – and another during the game when Milan defender Oguchi Onyewu was carried off with a torn knee tendon which sidelined him for months.

Coach Bob Bradley says: "It's a good thing that we respond and compete. These were hardly the circumstances we wanted but we showed our maturity and our team spirit."

That was not the only time the Americans showed their true grit. They trailed 2-0 to El Salvador in their second-final qualifier too. Young striker Jozy Altidore pulled one back and veteran Frankie Hejduk rescued a point in the 88th minute.

Bradley says: "We had mixed feelings afterwards. We knew we had things to work on. Yet we'd proved our mental toughness on a difficult day away from home."

The coach has rebuilt the squad after the international retirement of the likes of Claudio Reyna, Eddie Pope, Brad Friedel and Brian McBride.

Midfielder Landon Donovan — six times the domestic Player of the Year — is the undoubted star. Everton goalkeeper Tim Howard, skipper Carlos Bocanegra and Fulham forward Clint Dempsey add experience.

Bradley has blended them with emerging talents such as Onyewu, Hannover centre back Steve Cherundolo, Mönchengladbach midfielder Michael Bradley (the coach's son), Altidore and Houston Dynamos' defensive midfielder Ricardo Clark.

Bradley junior says: "When you look at all our players who are playing for good clubs in Europe, that's a very positive sign."

Howard says: "Basically, we're a young team with a lot of boldness. But we have a core group of experienced players who can push the younger players in the right direction."

Bocanegra adds: "It's an exciting time for us. We have a dynamic coach. The players are friends off the pitch, so we know each other well – and that shows in our performances."

The US always expect to reach the World Cup finals these days. They have appeared in every tournament since 1990, qualifying each time except for 1994, when they were hosts. They reached the quarter-finals in 2002, losing 1-0 to runners-up Germany.

Bradley's men had to negotiate some tricky moments en route to South Africa. They started with a 9-0 aggregate win over Barbados then comfortably topped a qualifying group including Trinidad and Tobago, Cuba and Guatemala.

Home form and home support were crucial. The US won eight of their nine qualifiers, including their first four in the final group.

Michael Bradley scored both goals – the second in stoppage time – as they opened with a 2-0 win over Mexico in Columbus. Recovery in El Salvador — followed by Altidore's hat trick in a 3-0 win over Trinidad and Tobago — put them in a strong position. Then they crashed 3-1 in Costa Rica.

Three days later, in Chicago, they trailed 1-0 to Carlos Costly's fourth minute goal for Honduras. Donovan levelled from the penalty spot after Mario Beata's handball. Bocanegra injured himself heading their 67th minute winner, diving low to head home Dempsey's flick. He says: "After we went behind, we were thinking; 'not again.' But we stayed together and fought back." A later victory over Honduras would seal their place in the finals.

As a "break" from the qualifiers, the US then did

United States' Carlos Bocanegra celebrates after scoring the winning goal against Honduras.

themselves proud in a South African warm-up — the 2009 Confederations Cup. Altidore and Dempsey scored to shock European champions Spain 2-0 in the semi-final. American energy overcame a technically superior team and inflicted Spain's first defeat in 35 matches.

Dempsey and Donovan even secured a 2-0 half-time lead over Brazil in the final. They fell away in the second half after Luis Fabiano scored within a minute. He netted another and Lucio grabbed an 84th-minute winner for the Brazilians.

Donovan said: "We've done better than we've ever done before at a competition like this. We've taken a step up. But we have to learn from what happened in the second half. We have to demand more from ourselves."

The US then succumbed 2-1 to Mexico in the Estadio Azteca after Davies had given them an early lead. Critics wondered what the Americans had learned. Others pointed out that Costa Rica, in 2001, were the only away team to win a World Cup qualifier in Mexico City.

It took a sprint from behind again — with goals from Altidore and Dempsey — to beat El Salvador 2-1 on September 5. Four days later, Clark grabbed the winner against Trinidad in Port of Spain.

That left the Americans needing three points against Honduras to reach South Africa. Honduras had won eight qualifiers in a row at home. Dempsey was injured. Eight US players were on one yellow card and treading a tightrope of suspension. Bradley felt they had to finish the job before facing Costa Rica.

He says: "We understood the challenge. This game meant everything to Honduras. The atmosphere in the stadium was passionate. But we understood the responsibility on us and were excited about finishing the job."

The Americans showed their determination again – and had a huge slice of luck. Julio De Leon gave Honduras a 47th-minute lead. Conor Casey headed the US level and finished off Donovan's pass for their second. Donovan made it 3-1 from a free kick. De Leon pulled a goal back. Then Jonathan Spector conceded a late penalty for hand ball – and Honduras's all-time top scorer Carlos Pavon fired over the bar. The 3-2 victory sent Bradley, Donovan and Co off to South Africa.

Their fightback against Costa Rica had ensured they finished top of the group while Mexico were drawing 2-2 in Trinidad.

Michael Bradley, who scored the first goal against Costa Rica, says: "It's great. I think we've seen in this cycle that CONCACAF has got a lot stronger. Honduras, Costa Rica, Mexico and us — it's been a battle. So, to finish first was a great achievement."

PROFILE OF THE 2010 US TEAM

Bob Bradley's United States set down a marker for their World Cup campaign when they beat free-flowing European champions Spain and then lost narrowly to Brazil in the final of the Confederations Cup in South Africa last June.

The unexpectedly strong American performances evidenced how a well-organised outfit can add up to even more than the sum of its individual parts.

Sunil Gulati, president of the United States Soccer Federation, says: "I'm proud of the record of all our national teams — the senior team, all the youth levels and the women — in qualifying for the finals of just about every world championship which comes around. Very few countries have a record that can stack up that way.

"It's particularly remarkable when you consider that though we have many players with European clubs, we don't have one US player in one of the very top Champions League clubs."

One US player who is on the books of an undoubted European giant could miss out on the World Cup along with promising Sochaux striker Charlie Davies, badly hurt in an October car crash.

Oguchi Onyewu's domineering displays in central defence in that Confederations Cup run earned him a transfer from Belgium's Standard Liège to Italian giants AC Milan. Yet he had yet to make his Serie A debut when a tendon injury cruelly ruled him out of much of the rest of the 2009-2010 season and threatened his prospects of playing again in South Africa.

Until that setback, Onyewu had been rehabilitating a reputation damaged by an unhappy spell in England with Newcastle United and his raw performances at the 2006 World Cup.

Four years after reaching the quarter-finals in South Korea and Japan, the US crashed out of the 2006 competition in the first round.

They managed just one point from three games, even if that did come against the eventual champions in a match the Americans ended with nine men, the Italians 10. Coach Bruce Arena lost his job not long afterwards, to be replaced by Bradley.

Donovan, however, was perhaps the man who bore the brunt of abuse from disappointed American fans, despite being the fourth youngest footballer to reach a century of international appearances.

Yet after enduring a second unhappy stint in European soccer, attacking midfielder Donovan has regained some credibility over the most recent US Major League Soccer season.

He was crowned Most Valuable Player at the end of the 2009 season, in which his LA Galaxy side were unlucky to lose the MLS Cup final against Real Salt Lake on penalties. Those rave reviews helped make up for the start of 2009, when he could barely get a game during a loan spell with Bayern Munich.

The experienced Landon Donovan will be without doubt one of the key men for the United States at the 2010 World Cup.

Bayern's reserve team coach Hermann Gerland even suggested Donovan was fit only for the club's third team.

After playing only seven games for Germany's Bayer Leverkusen between 2001 and 2005, he enjoyed better times only when returning home on loan to San Jose Earthquakes and then moving on to Los Angeles.

Another American seeking fame and fortune in Europe is striker Jozy Altidore, US football's most exciting starlet — and most expensive export.

He cost Spanish club Villareal £6m on joining from New York Red Bull in summer 2008. Yet he played only six times for the "Yellow Submarine" before being loaned out to Hull City in England.

His international scoring form has been eye-catching. The 6ft 1in striker, who made his MLS debut aged just 16, captured attention with four goals at the 2008 World Under-20 Youth Cup — including both US strikes in a 2-1 victory over Brazil.

Altidore scored six times in 2010 qualifying and he was followed in the US rankings by Clint Dempsey, with five, and Donovan, Chinese-American Brian Ching and coach's son Michael Bradley, with four apiece.

Altidore's haul included all three in a 3-0 triumph over Trinidad and Tobago. Yet it was Bradley's brace, in a 2-0 win over old rivals Mexico, which set off the US qualifying campaign to the perfect start.

Combative central midfielder Bradley has shrugged off any early allegations of nepotism to not only justify his place in the line-up, but frequently drive the whole team forward.

He plays in Germany, for Borussia Mönchengladbach, after impressing at Dutch club Heerenveen between 2006 and 2008.

Yet the key concern surrounding him is not his goalscoring, but his temperament — sometimes proving just too combustible. He was sent-off in the semi-final of the 2007 CONCACAF Gold Cup, against Canada, missing the Americans' triumph over Mexico in the final.

He was dismissed again in the 2009 Confederations Cup, against Spain — and earned himself an extra three-match ban for angrily confronting the officials after the final whistle.

One central midfielder who did make it to the final against Brazil, the nation of his birth, was Benny Feilhaber, formerly of Hamburg and Derby County but now playing in Denmark for Aarhus-based AGF.

Winger Dempsey is another US star who has finally settled down to regular starting football in England with his Fulham team. His Confederations Cup performances, and goals — one against Spain, and another against Brazil — won him an award for third-best player at the competition.

Clint Dempsey celebrates scoring the opening goal against Brazil during their Confederations Cup final soccer match.

A former team-mate at Fulham was US captain Carlos Bocanegra, now at Rennes for whom one of his rare goals helped win the 2009 French Cup final. Like Donovan and Glasgow Rangers forward DaMarcus Beasley, Bocanegra is a veteran of both the 2002 and 2006 World Cup campaigns.

He offers reliability as well as leadership and the versatility that can place him on the left or in the centre of defence, or even at times as a defensive midfield shield.

Fighting it out to start at right back could be West Ham United's former Manchester United youngster Jonathan Spector and Hannover's pacy Steve Cherundolo. Spector's surges forward and searching crosses set up Dempsey's Confederations Cup goals against both Egypt and Brazil.

Another attacking threat could come from left-back Jonathan Bernstein, whose stoppage-time equalizer against Costa Rica in October 2009 sealed the Americans' place in the finals — and consigned their opponents to a doomed play-off against Uruguay.

Backing up the back line is likely to be another former Manchester United man in goalkeeper Tim Howard, who has proved solid for both the national team and English 2009 FA Cup finalists Everton. Pushing him hard are Aston Villa's Brad Guzan and Wolverhampton Wanderers' Marcus Hahnemann.

GREAT US WORLD CUP MOMENTS

Talk about soccer as a "modern" American sport is to ignore history. The US compete at the finals in 2010 for the ninth time, stretching back to the historic, inaugural finals in Uruguay in 1930.

With no overnight jet flights 80 years ago, the US 1930 squad sailed from New Jersey in the *SS Munargo* on June 13 and finally arrived — via Bermuda, Rio de Janeiro and Santos — in rain-sodden Montevideo on July 1, a full 18 days after setting out.

Their first match against Belgium was also only the second match of the tournament — and hence in the entire history of the World Cup. US team manager Wilfred Cummings wrote: "The field [was] a bed of wet sticky clay with pools of water too numerous to count . . . We were greeted by a light snow storm, the first to fall in Montevideo for five years."

The Americans — nicknamed the Shot-Putters by the French for their size and strength — made a nervous start then hit their game to win 3-0 after opening the scoring with a long-range drive from Bart McGhee on the half hour. Skipper Thomas Florie and Bert Patenaude scored the others.

Another 3-0 win, this time against Paraguay, qualified the US as group winners for the semi-finals. Patenaude scored all three goals, the first hat-trick in the history of the World Cup.

Playing for the first time in the massive new Centenario stadium brought the US no luck. They were drawn against mighty Argentina, lost Ralph Tracy to a broken leg after 19 minutes in the days before substitutes and lost 6-1. The US were down to eight fit men when Jimmy Brown scored their last-minute consolation.

They were back again in 1934 in Italy in what, today, would be considered peculiar circumstances. The US were already in Rome when they played their one qualifying match. Aldo Donelli scored all the goals which brought a 4-2 win over Mexico. The subsequent finals campaign ended, however, after just 90 minutes and a 7-1 thrashing by their Italian hosts.

Some 16 years passed before the US again appeared at the finals. They finished runners-up in qualifying to Mexico but both went to the 1950 finals in Brazil and into a group along with Spain, Chile and joint favorites England.

Claims that the US team was made up largely of other countries' drop-outs were unfounded. Eight of the team who faced England had been born in the US; the non-US-born trio were Joe Maca (Belgium), Ed McIlvenny (Scotland) and Joe Gaetjens (Haiti).

They opened with a 3-1 defeat by Spain then sprang up what remains one of the great shocks of the World Cup by defeating England 1-0 in Belo Horizonte. One newspaper refused to print the score, believing it a misprint for 10-1.

Gaetjens headed the winner in the 37th minute in virtually the Americans' only attack. England hit the bar, the posts and found keeper Frank Borghi from St Louis in the form of his life. It was too much for even legends such as Tom Finney, Stan Mortensen, Wilf Mannion, Billy Wright and Alf Ramsey.

Next game the US crashed 5-2 to Chile — and would not be seen again at the finals for 40 years.

By the time Bob Gansler took his squad to Italy in 1990 the game had been changed almost beyond recognition. Jet travel and floodlighting had facilitated the dramatic impact of international midweek club soccer; television and sponsorship had revolutionized the game's finance; and Pele, Cosmos and the North American Soccer League had raised the US game's visibility.

Still, only a handful of the squad were developing their game within European club soccer and the US' tactical and technical naivety was punished 5-1 by Czechoslovakia, 1-0 by hosts Italy and 2-1 by Austria.

An underlying worry accompanied the squad home. FIFA had decided to take the finals to the US in 1994. Critics claimed it was a decision based on the values of commerce not sport because the US were barely competitive at world level.

One of Team USA's star players of 1994, Alexi Lalas keeps pace with Columbia star Faustino Asprilla.

All credit then to Alan Rothenberg, president of the USSF. He brought in Yugoslav master-coach Bora Milutinovic to make the most of the emergence of talent such as Tony Meola in goal, Paul Caligiuri in defense and Tab Ramos and John Harkes in midfield was complemented by characters such as guitar-strumming central defender Alexi Lalas.

The minimum requirement was to reach the knockout stages. Team America did so. Once more they created history, by hosting the first-ever indoor game in the finals, a 1-1 draw against Switzerland in the Pontiac Silverdome, Detroit.

Next time out came a 2-1 win in the Pasadena Rose Bowl over a Colombia team who never lived up to the promise of Cup-winning contenders. Worse, central defender Andres Escobar was shot dead when he returned home. Apparently he fell victim to a gambler who had lost a fortune betting on the game in which the hapless Escobar had put through his own goal to put the US on the way to a 2-1 victory.

A subsequent 1-0 defeat by Romania allowed the US to squeeze into the second round. They lost, unsurprisingly, to Brazil. But they had progressed beyond the group stage. For Milutinovic and Co it was mission accomplished.

The US have been at the finals of every World Cup since. In 1998 they featured in a remarkable game in Lyon against Iran at the height of political tension between the nations. The players, to their credit, put on a dramatic, sporting show in which the US were in no way discredited by the 2-1 defeat. Unfortunately they also lost to Germany and Yugoslavia and finished bottom of the group.

Bottom of the group was also their fate in Germany in 2006. In between, however, the US achieved their finest modern effort by reaching the 2002 quarter-finals in South Korea and Japan.

By now a new generation of talent had emerged in the likes of keeper Brad Friedel to forwards DaMarcus Beasley, Brian McBride and — above all — Landon Donovan.

They raced thrillingly 3-0 up against highly-fancied Portugal then clung on to win 3-2; they withstood a noisy battering from home fans to draw 1-1 with Korea; and a 3-1 defeat by Poland could not prevent them progressing into the second round and a CONCACAF "derby" with Mexico.

The Mexicans drew a fatal over-confidence from history. To their own fury and embarrassment they were outrun and, ultimately, outplayed. McBride and Donovan struck decisively.

Donovan also kept Germany keeper Oliver Kahn busy in the quarter-final. But luck went missing. The US and Gregg Berhalter were denied a penalty for handball by an unsighted referee and Donovan was denied time and again by an alert Kahn. At the other end Michael Ballack sneaked the only goal.

"Whoever invented football should be worshipped as a god." HUGO SANCHEZ

WELCOME TO THE 2010 WORLD CUP

AFRICA BECOMES A WORLD CUP HOST

Until 1994, the World Cup had been staged in Europe and Central and South America. Then the US hosted the tournament and it became a true World Cup. In 2010, history will be made when South Africa becomes Africa's first World Cup host.

Soccer's World Cup had been staged across much of the globe, the 18 previous finals being hosted by Uruguay in 1930, Italy (twice, in 1934 and 1990), France (also twice, in 1938 and 1998), Brazil (1950), Switzerland (1954), Sweden (1958), Chile (1962), England (1966), Mexico (twice, in 1970 and 1986), Germany (as West Germany in 1974 and as a unified country in 2006), Argentina (1978), Spain (1982), USA (1994) and Japan/Korea (2002). But Africa had yet to welcome the soccer world and that had to change. African countries had made bids previously, but they were all unsuccessful, with Morocco missing out for the 1994, 1998 and 2006 tournaments.

South Africa were also in the bidding process for the 2006 World Cup, but they were denied in controversial circumstances when, on the morning of the decisive final round of voting, one of their supporters, Charles Dempsey, the president of the Oceania Football Confederation, flew out before the meeting began, and left the country for family reasons. The vote, almost certain to end 12–12, would have gone South Africa's way on FIFA president Sepp Blatter's casting vote, instead it resulted in Germany winning.

African football's governing body, the CAF, was furious and their rage brought about an immediate change in FIFA policy. It was resolved that the World Cup hosting right would rotate to a different continent every four years. As Asia (Japan and South Korea) were hosts in 2002 and Europe (Gemany) had been awarded the rights for 2006, FIFA presdent Sepp Blatter's argument persuaded the executive committee to decide that Africa would get the World Cup in 2010 and South America in 2014. South Africa put in another bid, joined by Morocco, Egypt and, jointly, Libya and Tunisia.

The co-host bid was the first to fail, mainly because strong single-nation bids were on the table. Only one round of voting was necessary to decide a clear winner: South Africa polled 14 votes, Morocco 10 and Egypt none. South Africa would host the 2010 World Cup.

Winning the bid was just the first part. To fulfil the dreams of Nelson Mandela, Sepp Blatter and Danny Jordaan, the organizer of the bid, South Africa is going to have to put on a show for the 2010 FIFA World Cup, one that will grab the attention of fans visiting the country as well as the billions watching on television. Jordaan's aim and that of South Africa, too, is to produce what he hopes will be the best-ever World Cup. He stressed it was not only about soccer isssues, but to use the power of football in South Africa to re-engage with the world.

Jordaan admitted the organizing committee faced unique challenges, but he was confident that 2010 would come to be recognized as the time for soccer on the whole of the African continent.

Opposite: South African statesman Nelson Mandela's involvement helped secure the World Cup for South Africa.

Below: South Africa's fans are some of the most enthusiastic in the world and will bring a unique flavour to the World Cup.

A DIFFERENT WORLD CUP

The first World Cup to be held in Africa and the fifth World Cup to be played in the southern hemisphere, South Africa 2010 will bring new challenges for organisers, teams and fans.

Once South Africa had been awarded the 2010 World Cup the country entered into massive projects, not only to build or upgrade the stadiums, but also to provide the transportation and accommodation infrastructure. New airports, roads and rail lines have been built and this will assist the fans visiting South Africa in June and July, to say nothing of the millions of residents who will benefit in the years to come.

The statistics are sensational. The 2010 FIFA World Cup will attract some 450,000 foreign fans – out of a projected 21m visitors for the entire year – and more than £980m in broadcasting rights. Preparing for the finals and running them has created 150,000 new jobs and a profit is guaranteed despite massive expenditure, such as £55.5m on safety and security, some £1.2bn on stadium investment, £1.45bn on infrastructure and £800m on transport.

The head of the organizing committee, Danny Jordaan, travelled the world to gather advice and see how other countries worked to organize major events. He discovered that security remained a major concern and to counter this the number of police officers will rise from 175,000 to 200,000, with a reserve force of another 70,000. Supporting them will be helicopters, police control vehicles and mobile camera systems.

Jordaan says: "Security is the central issue underpinning the World Cup. Everyone coming here must have a safe, secure time so that they will want to return. Manchester United, Barcelona, Milan and big teams like these have all come here without a single incident. This is our track record. If we can keep secure 1.2m tourists in December, which is the major tourism period why can we not keep 450,000 secure during the FIFA World Cup?"

Justice will be swift for troublemakers with a network of "World Cup law courts" being created. Those arrested in or around the stadiums will be taken to the nearest designated police station, segregated from "ordinary" criminals, confronted by specially assigned prosecutors and possibly deported immediately.

FIFA have granted one special exemption from the rules about what can be brought into stadiums. Fans attending the 2010 World Cup will be able to bring vuvuzela trumpets into the stadia to create the unique atmosphere which enlivens big matches in South Africa. Those trumpets could be a crucial "12th man" for the hosts.

The noise created by these vuvuzelas appeared to upset the superstars who played in the 2009 Confederations Cup and if the same thing happens in 2010, then there may be a big smile on the face of Zukumi, the leopard character who is the official mascot for the 2010 World Cup. Zakumi will hope to match World Cup Willie (England, 1966), Tip & Tap (West Germany, 1974), Gauchito (Argentina,1978) and Footix (France, 1998) and bring South Africa glory on 11 July. Whatever happens, Zakumi and all of South Africa, will offer the world a welcoming smile.

Opposite: Brazil walked off with the 2009 Confederations Cup, but South Africa was praised for its immaculate organising of the event.

THE WORLD CUP VENUES

South Africa is a massive country – two-thirds larger in area than France, but with only two-thirds of the population – so there is much to see and do away from the stadiums.

For the tourist, South Africa offers an incredible range of activities, from wildlife-watching to lazing on some spectacular beaches. There are remarkable natural landscapes ranging from Table Mountain to the Kruger National Park, from the snowy peaks of the Drakensberg Range to the temperate valleys of Western Cape. And South Africa can boast about having three capital cities – Tschwane/Pretoria (executive), Mangaung/Bloemfontein (judicial, legal) and Cape Town (legislative) – and 11 official languages.

The organizers have been careful to make the World Cup accessible to South Africans and the ticket prices have been set at the lowest levels since 1990. South African residents can purchase group match tickets from as low as US$20, with tickets for the July 11 Final at Soccer City stadium costing US$150. For overseas fans, the cheapest tickets are US$80 and it will cost US$900 to watch the Final.

Ten stadiums in nine cities will stage the 64 matches and great care was taken to ensure the maximum number of local fans will be able to attend games. The host cities are in the north-east, east, centre, south and south-west of the country, but the majority of games will be in and around Johannesburg, South Africa's largest city and capital of the wealthiest province, Gauteng. It is the only city to have two stadiums, the famous Ellis Park and the brand new 92,000-capacity Soccer City. Other venues, such as Pretoria and Rustenburg, and even Nelspruit and Polokwane, are within striking distance by car or bus. Those fans looking to stay in Johannesburg wanting to go to Bloemfontein, Durban, and Port Elizabeth should look at the flight schedules.

The host nation is bordered by Namibia to the north-west, Botswana to the north, Zimbabwe to the north-east, Mozambique and Swaziland to the east and it envelops Lesotho. Every other point is ocean, the Atlantic on the west and the Indian to the south.

National and local authorities want football visitors to extend their stays to explore tourist attractions ranging from the southern coastline to the Kruger National Park. Promoting the country is, after all, one of the reasons such immense effort has been put into bringing the World Cup to Africa for the first time.

Opposite: Soccer City, Johannesburg has the honour of hosting the 2010 World Cup opening match and Final.

Below: A map of the 2010 World Cup venues

BLOEMFONTEIN

FREE STATE STADIUM
Capacity: 45,000
Matches: Six, including one second round.

Bloemfontein (or Mangaung – "the place of cheetahs") is nicknamed the "City of Roses." It is the capital of Free State Province and the country's judicial capital. At almost one mile (1,395m – 4,575 feet) above sea level, it does get cold at night and frosts are common.

CAPE TOWN

GREEN POINT STADIUM
Capacity: 64,000
Matches: Eight, including one second round, one quarter-final and one semi-final.

The second largest city in South Africa, Cape Town is the legislative capital, capital of Western Cape Province and the country's most popular tourist destination. This brand new Green Point stadium has the spectacular Table Mountain as its backdrop and will replace the Newlands rugby ground as the city's best sports venue.

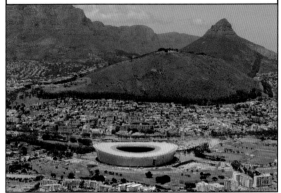

DURBAN

MOSES MABHIDA STADIUM
Capacity: 70,000
Matches: Seven, including one second round and one semi-final.

Durban is the busiest port in Africa and the largest city in the province of KwaZulu-Natal. The centrepiece of the Kings Park stadium precinct is the new Moses Mabhida Stadium. It boasts a spectacular arch to represent the unification of South Africa through sport.

JOHANNESBURG

SOCCER CITY
Capacity: 94,000
Matches: 8 including the opening match and the Final.

The largest football ground in South Africa, Soccer City is nicknamed the "Calabash", after the design of a traditional African brewing pot. The stadium replaces the old FNB Stadium, home of the South African FA's new office complex. Soccer City will be the focus on both June 11 and July 11.

JOHANNESBURG

ELLIS PARK
Capacity: 63,000
Matches: Seven, including one second round and one quarter-final.

Soccer fans will hope that history repeats itself in 2010 when Johannesburg hosts home World Cup success. In 1995 it was at Ellis Park where Nelson Mandela presented rugby captain Francois Pienaar with the trophy. Built in 1928 and named after a city councillor, Ellis Park hosted the 2009 Confederations Cup Final in which Brazil defeated the United States.

NELSPRUIT

MBOMBELA STADIUM
Capacity: 45,000
Matches: Five, all first round.

Nelspruit is a main stopover point for tourists travelling to the Kruger National Park and to Mozambique as well as being the capital of the Mpumalanga Province, formerly Eastern Transvaal. Located on the Crocodile River, it suggests going for a dip in it might be rather dangerous.

POLOKWANE

PETER MOKABA STADIUM
Capacity: 46,000
Matches: Four, all first round.

The most northerly of the host cities, Polokwane (formerly Pietersburg), the capital of Limpopo Province, has benefited from a new stadium for the 2010 World Cup, named after Peter Mokaba, a former leader of the African National Congress Youth League. Polokwane sits 1,230m (more than 4,000ft) above sea level so may be cold at night.

PORT ELIZABETH

NELSON MANDELA BAY STADIUM
Capacity: 47,000
Matches: Eight, including one second round, one quarter-final and the third-place play-off.

Port Elizabeth, on Nelson Mandela Bay in the Indian Ocean, considers itself the watersport capital of South Africa. It boasts a 40km (25 mile) stretch of golden beaches. The new stadium will be ready to showcase the World Cup in Eastern Cape Province.

PRETORIA

LOFTUS VERSFELD STADIUM
Capacity: 49,000
Matches: Six, including one second round.

Pretoria is the executive capital of South Africa and a rugby heartland – home to the Blue Bulls. Pretoria's Loftus Versfeld Stadium is more than 100 years old and it was named after Robert Owen Loftus Versfeld, the founder of organized sports in Pretoria. The city is also more than 1,200m (4,000ft) above sea level.

RUSTENBURG

ROYAL BAFOKENG STADIUM
Capacity: 45,000
Matches: Five, including one second round.

Rustenburg, known as the "Town of Rest" sits at the foot of the Magaliesberg mountain range in North West Province. Some US$50 million was spent in upgrading the Royal Bafokeng Stadium for the World Cup. The city is little more than an hour from Johannesburg on the way to the Botswana border.

South Africa put on a show for the 2009 Confederations Cup, which acted as a dress-rehearsal for the 2010 World Cup.

AN AMAZING EXPERIENCE

Soccer fans will recognize the atmosphere of the World Cup when they visit South Africa. But once they are seated in the stadium it will be a rather different experience.

Fans of clubs, such as the Mamelodi Sundowns, Orlando Pirates and Kaizer Chiefs are known for their spontaneity and seeing them rise to sing and dance in the seats and gangways is a regular event. But there will be a unique soundtrack to the 2010 World Cup finals: the vuvuzela. The instrument, a cross between a trumpet and an air horn, is a relatively new phenomenon in soccer. South Africa won the 1996 African Cup of Nations as hosts and, a year later, played in the Confederations. In both tournaments, South Africa's fans ensured that all their matches were played to a cacophony of sound from them.

FIFA was urged to ban the vuvuzela from stadiums and security experts warned that allowing them into the stadiums would contravene FIFA's own regulations about dangerous weapons. But they were allowed into the 2009 Confederations Cup and matches were played to the sound of thousands of these instruments producing an ear-splitting noise.

Some coaches and players at the Confederations Cup were put off by the raucous sound of thousands of vuvuzelas. Dunga of Brazil and Bert Van Marwijk of Holland both criticised the instruments' "distracting sound" and went as far as to say they thought that their players had been inconvenienced by the noise. However, FIFA decided that fans will be allowed to bring them into the stadiums at the World Cup. And it might just provide the advantage and motivation South Africa needs to produce some great shocks.

FIFA president, Sepp Blatter, observed: " It's a local sound and I don't know how it is possible to stop it. I always said that when we decided to go to South Africa it was because we wanted to be in Africa – not western Europe. Vuvuzelas are noisy but the crowds here have energy, rhythm, music, dance, drums. This is Africa. We have to adapt a little. Every country's fans have their music.

Come to Switzerland and you hear the fans ring cowbells. Maybe the vuvuzelas are louder but the principle is the same."

When they arrive at the ten venues, fans will discover how imaginative architects have brought that dream to life in some remarkable designs for the new stadia – such as the "giraffes" supporting the Mbembela Stadium roof in Nelspruit and the arch soaring over the Moses Mabhida Stadium in Durban.

Opposite: Crazy outfits, wild dancing and joyful singing are all part of watching soccer in South Africa.

Below: Vuvuzela horns will be a prominent feature of the World Cup and will bring a unique local sound to the tournament.

"Football is simple but the hardest thing to do is playing simple football." JOHAN CRUYFF

WORLD CUP QUALIFICATION

THE LONG JOURNEY TO THE FINALS

The 2010 World Cup is not just about the 64 matches in South Africa. The 31 visiting countries have played in a qualifying tournament that comprised 853 matches 2,344 goals and a combined attendance of more than 20 million fans.

The first match was played in front of just 60 fans on the Pacific island of Samoa on August 25, 2007, when the hosts lost 4–0 to Vanuatu. Richard Iwai scored the first goal after 21 minutes in Apia. Qualifying came to an end, 815 days later, in Montevideo, Uruguay, on November 18, 2009. The last goal, 16 minutes from the end of the final qualifying play-off match came from Walter Centeno of Costa Rica.

Europe, as usual, sent the most representatives to the World Cup finals, with 13. There were nine groups, with the winners qualifying automatically, along with the four runners-up, who triumphed in two-legged play-off matches. And, as always happens, there were many intriguing groups.

In Group 6, Croatia, who had knocked England out of the European Championships a year earlier, were drawn with them again, and with 2006 World Cup quarter-finalists Ukraine. Sweden had to see off Denmark and Portugal in Group 1. The Czech Republic faced Slovakia and Slovenia. Turkey and Belgium were pitted against European champions Spain and Bosnia-Herzegovina. Austria had to get past Serbia and France. They all failed, while Ukraine, Portugal, Slovenia, Bosnia-Herzegovina

and France joined Russia, the Republic of Ireland and Greece in the play-offs.

Spain were the most efficient qualifiers anywhere in the world, winning all 10 of their matches. England were close behind, with nine wins; their only defeat was to Ukraine when it no longer mattered, and they were the European section's 34-goal top scorers. Holland were also perfect in eight matches, while Germany and Italy topped their groups undefeated. The four other group winners were Switzerland, Serbia, Slovakia and Denmark.

The big surprise in South America was the struggle of Argentina to finish in the top four. Coached by Diego Maradona, a run of four defeats in five matches – including 6–1 in Bolivia – left them in danger of missing out of even a play-off place. But a stoppage time winner at home to Peru and a late strike from Mario Bolatti in Uruguay gave them a 1–0 victory and fourth place in the group, behind Brazil, Chile and Paraguay.

Africa has never had so many representatives at the finals. with five qualifiers joining hosts South Africa. It was a long and arduous journey, with three rounds including two group stages. For the first time since 1934, the hosts participated in the second round, but this was because it also served as the qualification for the January 2010 Africa Cup of Nations. South Africa finished 11 points behind Group 4 winners Nigeria, and level with Sierra Leone.

Twenty countries advanced to the five final qualifying groups. Cameroon reached their sixth finals, seeing off former finalists Morocco and Togo. Nigeria profited from Tunisia's last game

Left: New Zealand's 1-0 win over Bahrain in the qualifying play-off second leg meant the "All Whites" reached the World Cup for the first time since 1982.

Left: Russia and Germany met in Group 4 of the European qualifying competition. Germany ultimately topped the table, condemning Russia to the play-off against Slovenia.

defeat in Mozambique, Côte d'Ivoire brushed aside Burkina Faso, Malawi and Guinea, while Ghana were too strong for Benin, Mali and Sudan. The last group included African Cup of Nations record winners Egypt and Algeria, but they couldn't be split, both teams winning four and losing one of their six matches and both scored nine goals and conceded four. The qualification tournament rules decreed a play-off would decide the last country to advance.

Asia's qualifying tournament contained two rounds of two-legged ties followd by two rounds of group matches. The Confederation had been strengthened by the inclusion of former Oceania champions Australia and they justified their favourite status by finishing top of their final group ahead of Japan, who also advanced to South Africa.

South Korea topped the other final group, but there was a surprise runner-up. North Korea needed a draw in Riyadh, Saudi Arabia, to finish second in the group and they duly achieved it in a match which ended goalless.

The North and Central America and Caribbean tournament produced some shocks, but the United States and Mexico eventually clinched their places. A close battle for the final automatic spot went to Honduras, who denied Costa Rica, this after the Ticos conceded a goal four minutes into stoppage time against the USA to draw 2–2 in Washington DC.

Oceania's strongest nation, with Australia "defecting" to Asia, was New Zealand and the All Whites eased into a play-off with the winner of the first Asian play-off round. This was Bahrain, who surprised Saudi Arabia on away goals, a 2–2 draw in Riyadh following a goalless affair in Manama.

The African Confederation play-off was a one-off match, in Khartoum, Sudan. Egypt and Algeria produced a passionate affair and it was decided by a single goal, scored by Antar Yahia just before half-time.

Bahrain and New Zealand played out a goalless first leg in their play-off to give the All Whites a narrow advantage for the return in Wellington. In front of the largest crowd ever to watch a soccer match in New Zealand, Rory Fallon scored for the All Whites just before half-time and goalkeeper Mark Paston saved a penalty from Sayed Mohamed Adnan early in the second half to give New Zealand their first World Cup finals berth since 1982.

The play-off between Costa Rica and Uruguay, went to the 1930 and 1950 world champions, who won 1–0 in San Jose, with a goal from Diego Lugano and drew 1–1 in Montevideo. Walter Centeno scored four minutes after Sebastian Abreu to give Costa Rica hope, but it was not to be.

The four European play-off ties were all desperately close. Greece surprised Ukraine in Dontesk with a goal from Dimitrios Salpingidis and played out a goalless draw in the return. A pair of 1–0 wins were enough for Portugal to beat Bosnia-Herzegovina. The biggest shock saw Slovenia win on away goals against Russia, Nejc Pecnik scoring in the 88th minute in Moscow to make it 2–1 on the night and 2–2 on aggregate.

But the real drama and controversy came in the Stade de France, where Thierry Henry's handball went unseen by any of the officials and his cross was converted by William Gallas to make it 1–1 on the night against the Republic of Ireland, but 2–1 on aggregate to Les Bleus.

Henry admitted his guilt immediately after the game, and it created a firestorm of complaints and disapproval from the media and desperate Irish fans. Despite demands from the Football Association of Ireland and the Irish government, FIFA ruled that the result would stand and no replay would be permitted.

AFRICA

1st round

Madagascar bt **Comoros** 6-2, 4-0 (10-2 agg)
Sierra Leone bt **Guinea-Bissau** 1-0, 0-0 (1-0 agg)
Djibouti bt **Somalia** 1-0 (single game)

2nd round

Group 1

	P	W	D	L	F	A	Pts
Cameroon	6	5	1	0	14	2	16
Cape Verde Islands	6	3	0	3	7	8	9
Tanzania	6	2	2	2	9	6	8
Mauritius	6	0	1	5	3	17	1

Group 2

	P	W	D	L	F	A	Pts
Guinea	6	3	2	1	9	5	11
Kenya	6	3	1	2	8	5	10
Zimbabwe	6	1	3	2	4	6	6
Namibia	6	2	0	4	7	12	6

Group 3

	P	W	D	L	F	A	Pts
Benin	6	4	0	2	12	8	12
Angola	6	3	1	2	11	8	10
Uganda	6	3	1	2	8	9	10
Niger	6	1	0	5	5	11	3

Group 4

	P	W	D	L	F	A	Pts
Nigeria	6	6	0	0	11	1	18
South Africa	6	2	1	3	5	5	7
Sierra Leone	6	2	1	3	4	8	7
Equatorial Guinea	6	1	0	5	4	10	3

Group 5

	P	W	D	L	F	A	Pts
Ghana	6	4	0	2	11	5	12
Gabon	6	4	0	2	8	3	12
Libya	6	4	0	2	7	4	12
Lesotho	6	0	0	6	2	16	0

Group 6

	P	W	D	L	F	A	Pts
Algeria	6	3	1	2	7	4	10
Gambia	6	2	3	1	6	3	9
Senegal	6	2	3	1	9	7	9
Liberia	6	0	3	3	4	12	3

Group 7

	P	W	D	L	F	A	Pts
Côte d'Ivoire	6	3	3	0	10	2	12
Mozambique	6	2	2	2	7	5	8
Madagascar	6	1	3	2	2	7	6
Botswana	6	1	2	3	3	8	5

Group 8

	P	W	D	L	F	A	Pts
Morocco	4	3	0	1	11	5	9
Rwanda	4	3	0	1	7	3	9
Mauritania	4	0	0	4	2	12	0

Ethiopia expelled – record removed

Group 9

	P	W	D	L	F	A	Pts
Burkina Faso	6	5	1	0	14	5	16
Tunisia	6	4	1	1	11	3	13
Burundi	6	2	0	4	5	9	6
Seychelles	6	0	0	6	4	17	0

Group 10

	P	W	D	L	F	A	Pts
Mali	6	4	0	2	13	8	12
Sudan	6	3	0	3	9	9	9
Congo	6	3	0	3	7	8	9
Chad	6	2	0	4	7	11	6

Group 11

	P	W	D	L	F	A	Pts
Zambia	4	2	1	1	2	1	7
Togo	4	2	0	2	8	3	6
Swaziland	4	1	1	2	2	8	4

Group 12

	P	W	D	L	F	A	Pts
Egypt	6	5	0	1	13	2	15
Malawi	6	4	0	2	14	5	12
Congo DR	6	3	0	3	14	6	9
Djibouti	6	0	0	6	2	30	0

3rd round

Group A

	P	W	D	L	F	A	Pts
Cameroon	6	4	1	1	9	2	13
Gabon	6	3	0	3	9	7	9
Togo	6	2	2	2	3	7	8
Morocco	6	0	3	3	3	8	3

Group B

	P	W	D	L	F	A	Pts
Nigeria	6	3	3	0	9	4	12
Tunisia	6	3	2	1	7	4	11
Mozambique	6	2	1	3	3	5	7
Kenya	6	1	0	5	5	11	3

Group C

	P	W	D	L	F	A	Pts
Algeria	7	5	1	1	10	4	16
Egypt	7	4	1	2	9	5	13
Zambia	6	1	2	3	2	5	5
Rwanda	6	0	2	4	1	8	2

Group D

	P	W	D	L	F	A	Pts
Ghana	6	4	1	1	9	3	13
Benin	6	3	1	2	6	6	10
Mali	6	2	3	1	8	7	9
Sudan	6	0	1	5	2	9	1

Group E

	P	W	D	L	F	A	Pts
Côte d'Ivoire	6	5	1	0	19	4	16
Burkina Faso	6	4	0	2	10	11	12
Malawi	6	1	1	4	4	11	4
Guinea	6	1	0	5	7	14	3

Qualified: South Africa (hosts), Cameroon, Tunisia, Algeria, Ghana, Côte d'Ivoire

---

ASIA

1st round

Tajikistan bt **Bangladesh** 1-1, 5-0 (6-1 agg)
Thailand bt **Macau** 6-1, 7-1 (13-2 agg)
United Arab Emirates bt **Vietnam** 1-0, 5-0 (6-0 agg)
Syria bt **Afghanistan** 3-0, 2-1 (5-1 agg)
Singapore bt **Palestine** 4-0, 3-0 (7-0 agg)
Lebanon bt **India** 4-1, 2-2 (6-3 agg)
Oman bt **Nepal** 2-0, 2-0 (4-0 agg)

Togo defeated Cameroon 1-0 in qualifying. Here, Cameroon's Rigobert Song trips while challenging Togo's Alexys Romao.

Yemen bt **Maldives** 3-0, 0-2 (3-2 agg)
Turkmenistan bt **Cambodia** 1-0, 4-1 (5-1 agg)
Uzbekistan bt **Chinese Taipei** 9-0, 2-0 (11-0 agg)
Jordan bt **Kyrgyzstan** 0-2, 2-0 (2-2 agg, 6-5 pens)
North Korea bt **Mongolia** 4-1, 5-1 (9-2 agg)
Hong Kong bt **Timor-Leste** 3-2, 8-1 (11-3 agg)
Qatar bt **Sri Lanka** 1-0, 5-0 (6-0 agg)
Bahrain bt **Malaysia** 4-1, 0-0 (4-1 agg)
China PR bt **Myanmar** 7-0, 4-0 (11-0 agg)
Iraq bt **Pakistan** 7-0, 0-0 (7-0 agg)

2nd round

Thailand bt **Yemen** 1-1, 1-0 (2-1 agg)
Singapore bt **Tajikistan** 2-0, 1-1 (3-1 agg)
Syria bt **Indonesia** 4-1, 7-0 (11-1 agg)
Turkmenistan bt **Hong Kong** 3-0, 0-0 (3-0 agg)

3rd round

Group 1

	P	W	D	L	F	A	Pts
Australia	6	3	1	2	7	3	10
Qatar	6	3	1	2	5	6	10
Iraq	6	2	1	3	4	6	7
China PR	6	1	3	2	3	4	6

Group 2

	P	W	D	L	F	A	Pts
Japan	6	4	1	1	12	3	13
Bahrain	6	3	2	1	7	5	11
Oman	6	2	2	2	5	7	8
Thailand	6	0	1	5	5	14	1

Group 3

	P	W	D	L	F	A	Pts
South Korea	6	3	3	0	10	3	12
North Korea	6	3	3	0	4	0	12
Jordan	6	2	1	3	6	6	7
Turkmenistan	6	0	1	5	1	12	1

Group 4

	P	W	D	L	F	A	Pts
Saudi Arabia	6	5	0	1	15	5	15
Uzbekistan	6	5	0	1	17	7	15
Singapore	6	2	0	4	7	16	6
Lebanon	6	0	0	6	3	14	0

Group 5

	P	W	D	L	F	A	Pts
Iran	6	3	3	0	7	2	12
UAE	6	2	2	2	7	7	8
Syria	6	2	2	2	7	8	8
Kuwait	6	1	1	4	8	12	4

4th round

Group 1

	P	W	D	L	F	A	Pts
Australia	8	6	2	0	12	1	20
Japan	8	4	3	1	11	6	15
Bahrain	8	3	1	4	6	8	10
Qatar	8	1	3	4	5	14	6
Uzbekistan	8	1	1	6	5	10	4

Group 2

	P	W	D	L	F	A	Pts
South Korea	8	4	4	0	12	4	16
North Korea	8	3	3	2	7	5	12
Saudi Arabia	8	3	3	2	8	8	12
Iran	8	2	5	1	8	7	11
UAE	8	0	1	7	6	17	1

Qualified: Australia, Japan, South Korea, North Korea

Play-offs: Bahrain, Saudi Arabia

CONCACAF

(Confederation of North, Central American and Caribbean Association Football)

1st round

Barbados bt **Dominica** 1-1, 1-0 (2-1 agg)
St Lucia bt **Turks & Caicos** 1-2, 2-0 (3-2 agg)
Bermuda bt **Cayman Islands** 1-1, 3-1 (4-2 agg)
Antigua & Barbuda bt **Aruba** 3-0, 1-0 (4-0 agg)
Belize bt **St Kitts & Nevis** 3-1, 1-1 (4-2 agg)
Bahamas bt **British Virgin Islands** 1-1, 2-2 (3-3 agg, away goals)
Puerto Rico bt **Dominican Rep.** 1-0 (single game)
Grenada bt **US Virgin Islands** 10-0 (single game)
Surinam bt **Montserrat** 7-1 (single game)
El Salvador bt **Anguilla** 12-0, 4-0 (16-0 agg)
Netherlands Antilles bt **Nicaragua** 1-0, 2-0 (3-0 agg)

2nd round

United States bt **Barbados** 8-0, 1-0 (9-0 agg)
Guatemala bt **St Lucia** 6-0, 3-1 (9-1 agg)
Trinidad & Tobago bt **Bermuda** 1-2, 2-0 (3-2 agg)
Cuba bt **Antigua & Barbuda** 4-3, 4-0 (8-3 agg)
Mexico bt **Belize** 2-0, 7-0 (9-0 agg)
Jamaica bt **Bahamas** 7-0, 6-0 (13-0 agg)
Honduras bt **Puerto Rico** 4-0, 2-2 (6-2 agg)
Canada bt **St Vincent & Grenadines** 3-0, 4-1 (7-1 agg)
Costa Rica bt **Grenada** 2-2, 3-0 (5-2 agg)
Surinam bt **Guyana** 1-0, 2-1 (3-1 agg)
El Salvador bt **Panama** 3-1 (3-2 agg)
Haiti bt **Netherlands Antilles** 0-0, 1-0 (1-0 agg)

3rd round

Group 1

	P	W	D	L	F	A	Pts
United States	6	5	0	1	14	3	15
Trinidad & Tobago	6	3	2	1	9	6	11
Guatemala	6	1	2	3	6	7	5
Cuba	6	1	0	5	5	18	3

Group 2

	P	W	D	L	F	A	Pts
Honduras	6	4	0	2	9	5	12
Mexico	6	3	1	2	9	6	10
Jamaica	6	3	1	2	6	6	10
Canada	6	0	2	4	6	13	2

Group 3

	P	W	D	L	F	A	Pts
Costa Rica	6	6	0	0	20	3	18
El Salvador	6	3	1	2	11	4	10
Haiti	6	0	3	3	4	13	3
Surinam	6	0	2	4	4	19	2

4th round

	P	W	D	L	F	A	Pts
United States	10	6	2	2	19	13	20
Mexico	10	6	1	3	18	12	19
Honduras	10	5	1	4	17	11	16
Costa Rica	10	5	1	4	15	15	16
El Salvador	10	2	2	6	9	15	8
Trinidad & Tobago	10	1	3	6	10	22	6

Qualified: United States, Mexico, Honduras

Play-offs: Costa Rica

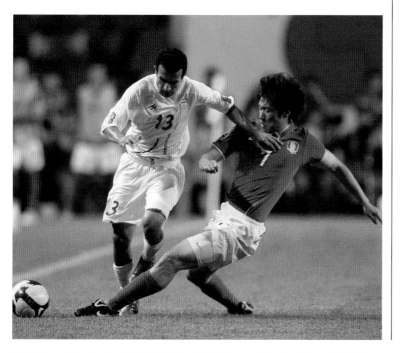

South Korea's Manchester United midfielder Park Ji-Sung tackles Iran's Hossein Kaebi in their Asian qualifying match.

EUROPE

Group 1

	P	W	D	L	F	A	Pts
Denmark	10	6	3	1	16	5	21
Portugal	10	5	4	1	17	5	19
Sweden	10	5	3	2	13	5	18
Hungary	10	5	1	4	10	8	16
Albania	10	1	4	5	6	13	7
Malta	10	0	1	9	0	26	1

Group 2

	P	W	D	L	F	A	Pts
Switzerland	10	6	3	1	18	8	21
Greece	10	6	2	2	20	10	20
Latvia	10	5	2	3	18	15	17
Israel	10	4	4	2	20	10	16
Luxembourg	10	1	2	7	4	25	5
Moldova	10	0	3	7	6	18	3

Group 3

	P	W	D	L	F	A	Pts
Slovakia	10	7	1	2	22	10	22
Slovenia	10	6	2	2	18	4	20
Czech Republic	10	4	4	2	17	6	16
Northern Ireland	10	4	3	3	13	9	15
Poland	10	3	2	5	19	14	11
San Marino	10	0	0	10	1	47	0

Group 4

	P	W	D	L	F	A	Pts
Germany	10	8	2	0	26	5	26
Russia	10	7	1	2	19	6	22
Finland	10	5	3	2	14	14	18
Wales	10	4	0	6	9	12	12
Azerbaijan	10	1	2	7	4	14	5
Liechtenstein	10	0	2	8	2	23	2

Group 5

	P	W	D	L	F	A	Pts
Spain	10	10	0	0	28	5	30
Bosnia-Herzegovina	10	6	1	3	25	13	19
Turkey	10	4	3	3	13	10	15
Belgium	10	3	1	6	13	20	10
Estonia	10	2	2	6	9	24	8
Armenia	10	1	1	8	6	22	4

Group 6

	P	W	D	L	F	A	Pts
England	10	9	0	1	34	6	27
Ukraine	10	6	3	1	21	6	21
Croatia	10	6	2	2	19	13	20
Belarus	10	4	1	5	19	14	13
Kazakhstan	10	2	0	8	11	29	6
Andorra	10	0	0	10	3	39	0

Group 7

	P	W	D	L	F	A	Pts
Serbia	10	7	1	2	22	8	22
France	10	6	3	1	18	9	21
Austria	10	4	2	4	14	15	14
Lithuania	10	4	0	6	10	11	12
Romania	10	3	3	4	12	18	12
Faroe Islands	10	1	1	8	5	20	4

Group 8

	P	W	D	L	F	A	Pts
Italy	10	7	3	0	18	7	24
Republic of Ireland	10	4	6	0	12	8	18
Bulgaria	10	3	5	2	17	13	14
Cyprus	10	2	3	5	14	16	9
Montenegro	10	1	6	3	9	14	9
Georgia	10	0	3	7	7	19	3

Group 9

	P	W	D	L	F	A	Pts
Netherlands	8	8	0	0	17	2	24
Norway	8	2	4	2	9	7	10
Scotland	8	3	1	4	6	11	10
FYR Macedonia	8	2	1	5	5	11	7
Iceland	8	1	2	5	7	13	5

Qualified: Denmark, Switzerland, Slovakia, Germany, Spain, England, Serbia, Italy, Netherlands

Play-offs: Portugal, Greece, Slovenia, Russia, Bosnia-Herzegovina, Ukraine, France, Republic of Ireland

Portugal's midfield maestro Deco takes on Bosnia-Herzegovina's Samir Muratovic in their European qualifying play-off match.

OCEANIA

1st round

Group 1

	P	W	D	L	F	A	Pts
Fiji	3	2	1	0	9	1	7
New Caledonia	3	2	1	0	5	1	7
Tahiti	3	1	0	2	1	5	3
Tuvalu	0	0	0	0	0	0	0
Cook Islands	3	0	0	3	0	8	0

Associate Members, Tuvalu's results not included as part of 2010 World Cup qualifying.

Group 2

	P	W	D	L	F	A	Pts
Solomon Islands	4	4	0	0	21	1	12
Vanuatu	4	3	0	1	23	3	9
Samoa	4	2	0	2	9	8	6
Tonga	4	1	0	3	6	10	3
American Samoa	4	0	0	4	1	38	0

Final round

Group 3

	P	W	D	L	F	A	Pts
New Zealand	6	5	0	1	14	5	15
New Caledonia	6	2	2	2	12	10	8
Fiji	6	2	1	3	8	11	7
Vanuatu	6	1	1	4	5	13	4

Play-offs: New Zealand

SOUTH AMERICA

Group 1

	P	W	D	L	F	A	Pts
Brazil	18	9	7	2	33	11	34
Chile	18	10	3	5	32	22	33
Paraguay	18	10	3	5	24	16	33
Argentina	18	8	4	6	23	20	28
Uruguay	18	6	6	6	28	20	24
Ecuador	18	6	5	7	22	26	23
Colombia	18	6	5	7	14	18	23
Venezuela	18	6	4	8	23	29	22
Bolivia	18	4	3	11	22	36	15
Peru	18	3	4	11	11	34	13

Qualified: Brazil, Chile, Paraguay, Argentina

Play-offs: Uruguay

PLAY-OFFS

Asia
Bahrain bt **Saudi Arabia** 0-0, 2-2 (2-2 agg, away goals)

Asia v Oceania
New Zealand bt **Bahrain** 0-0, 1-0 (1-0 agg)

S America v CONCACAF
Uruguay bt **Costa Rica** 1-0, 1-1 (2-1 agg)

Europe
Greece bt **Ukraine** 0-0, 1-0 (1-0 agg)
Portugal bt **Bosnia-Herzegovina** 1-0, 1-0 (2-0 agg)
France bt **Republic of Ireland** 1-0, 1-1 (2-1 agg)
Slovenia bt **Russia** 1-2, 1-0 (2-2 agg, away goals)

New Zealand eventually triumphed over Bahrain in a closely contested World Cup play-off match to secure their place in South Africa.

THE WORLD CUP 2010 FINALS DRAW

The players, officials and fans of the 2010 qualifying teams all want to be at Soccer City, Johannesburg, on July 11, 2010, playing in the Final. It all started in December 2009, with the draw for the Finals.

The draw is a spectacular event to whet everyone's appetite for the main event six months later and it was no different in Cape Town on December 4, 2009. The draw was conducted by FIFA president Sepp Blatter, FIFA general secretary Jerome Valcke, England footballer David Beckham and South African actress Charlize Theron. Their first task was to allocate groups to the eight top seeds and they were as follows: South Africa (A), Argentina (B), England (C), Germany (D), The Netherlands (E), Italy (F), Brazil (G) and Spain (H).

Then came the other 24 teams, allocated into the eight groups and it created many talking points with some famous rivalries renewed. These included England against the United States, Portugal against both Brazil and North Korea and a repeat of the 1966 first round when the hosts faced Mexico, Uruguay and France. Thus South Africa will open up the tournament at 4.00 pm local time on June 11, at Soccer City, Johannesburg, against Mexico, who are always awkward opponents at a World Cup.

After the draw, European champions Spain were rated by the London bookmakers as favourites to win the World Cup. Coach Vicente Del Bosque was not unnerved by the draw and said: "We can't complain. We can't hide the fact we are one of the favourites to win. We will have had a long season but we will have plenty of time to rest and to prepare."

Diego Maradona, coach of Argentina and trying to become the second man – after Franz Beckenbauer – to captain and coach World Cup winners, felt good and bad omens as Argentina were drawn in Group B against South Korea, Nigeria and Greece. He played against South Korea in 1986 when Argentina went on to win the tournament, but failed a dope test after playing against Nigeria and was kicked out of the 1994 finals.

England coach Fabio Capello was cautiously confident after the draw matched England with the United States, Algeria and Slovenia in Group C. He will not want a repeat of England's 1–0 defeat against the part-timers from the United States in 1950, one of the biggest shocks in the history of the World Cup. And this time the USA already have experienced local conditions at the 2009 Confederations Cup.

Other under-pressure managers at the draw included Germany boss Joachim Löw and the Netherland's Bert Van Marwijk. They sought to defuse over-confidence among fans back home while Italy's Marcello Lippi and Brazil's Dunga feared complacency among their own players.

In response to this Dunga said: "The toughest match is going to be the first one . . . then the second one . . . and then the third one. That is the way we think. It's the only way we know."

Opposite: The World Cup draw in December 2009 signalled the countdown to the World Cup finals, with teams finding out their opening opponents.

Below: The World Cup draw was a star-studded affair and attended by English footballer David Beckham and South African actress Charlize Theron.

WORLD CUP FILL-IN CHART

GROUP A

11-JUN-10	15:00 BST	JOHANNESBURG (JSC)	
SOUTH AFRICA		**MEXICO**	
11-JUN-10	19:30 BST	CAPE TOWN	
URUGUAY		**FRANCE**	
16-JUN-10	19:30 BST	PRETORIA	
SOUTH AFRICA		**URUGUAY**	
17-JUN-10	12:30 BST	POLOKWANE	
FRANCE		**MEXICO**	
22-JUN-10	15:00 BST	RUSTENBURG	
MEXICO		**URUGUAY**	
22-JUN-10	15:00 BST	BLOEMFONTEIN	
FRANCE		**SOUTH AFRICA**	

GROUP B

12-JUN-10	12:30 BST	PORT ELIZABETH	
SOUTH KOREA		**GREECE**	
12-JUN-10	15:00 BST	JOHANNESBURG (JEP)	
ARGENTINA		**NIGERIA**	
17-JUN-10	12:30 BST	JOHANNESBURG (JSC)	
ARGENTINA		**SOUTH KOREA**	
17-JUN-10	15:00 BST	BLOEMFONTEIN	
GREECE		**NIGERIA**	
22-JUN-10	19:30 BST	DURBAN	
NIGERIA		**SOUTH KOREA**	
22-JUN-10	19:30 BST	POLOKWANE	
GREECE		**ARGENTINA**	

GROUP C

12-JUN-10	19:30 BST	RUSTENBURG	
ENGLAND		**USA**	
13-JUN-10	12:30 BST	POLOKWANE	
ALGERIA		**SLOVENIA**	
18-JUN-10	15:00 BST	JOHANNESBURG (JEP)	
SLOVENIA		**USA**	
18-JUN-10	19:30 BST	CAPE TOWN	
ENGLAND		**ALGERIA**	
23-JUN-10	15:00 BST	PORT ELIZABETH	
SLOVENIA		**ENGLAND**	
23-JUN-10	15:00 BST	PRETORIA	
USA		**ALGERIA**	

GROUP D

13-JUN-10	15:00 BST	PRETORIA	
SERBIA		**GHANA**	
13-JUN-10	19:30 BST	DURBAN	
GERMANY		**AUSTRALIA**	
18-JUN-10	12:30 BST	PORT ELIZABETH	
GERMANY		**SERBIA**	
19-JUN-10	15:00 BST	RUSTENBURG	
GHANA		**AUSTRALIA**	
23-JUN-10	19:30 BST	JOHANNESBURG (JSC)	
GHANA		**GERMANY**	
23-JUN-10	19:30 BST	NELSPRUIT	
AUSTRALIA		**SERBIA**	

ROUND OF 16

(1)	26-JUN-10	15:00 BST	PORT ELIZABETH
1A			**2B**
(3)	26-JUN-10	19:30 BST	RUSTENBURG
1C			**2D**
(4)	27-JUN-10	15:00 BST	BLOEMFONTEIN
1D			**2C**
(2)	27-JUN-10	19:30 BST	JOHANNESBURG (JSC)
1B			**2A**

(5)	28-JUN-10	15:00 BST	DURBAN
1E			**2F**
(7)	28-JUN-10	19:30 BST	JOHANNESBURG (JEP)
1G			**2H**
(6)	29-JUN-10	15:00 BST	PRETORIA
1F			**2E**
(8)	29-JUN-10	19:30 BST	CAPE TOWN
1H			**2G**

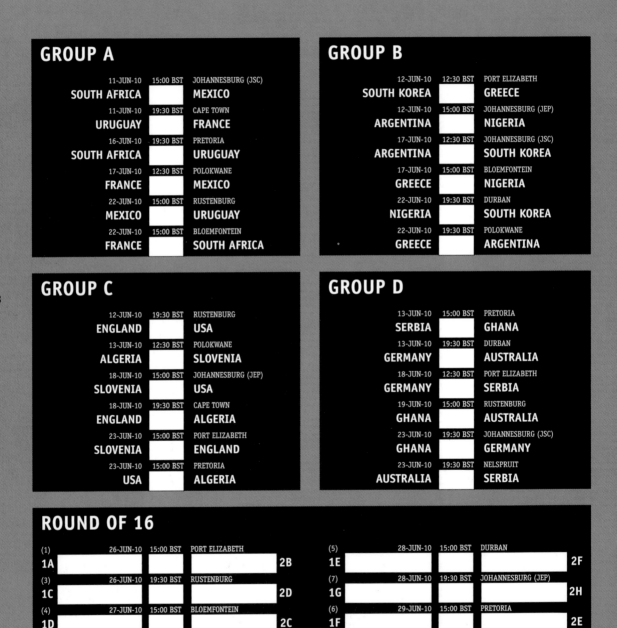

GROUP E

Date	Time	Venue	Team 1		Team 2
14-JUN-10	12:30 BST	JOHANNESBURG (JSC)	NETHERLANDS		DENMARK
14-JUN-10	15:00 BST	BLOEMFONTEIN	JAPAN		CAMEROON
19-JUN-10	12:30 BST	DURBAN	NETHERLANDS		JAPAN
19-JUN-10	19:30 BST	PRETORIA	CAMEROON		DENMARK
24-JUN-10	19:30 BST	RUSTENBURG	DENMARK		JAPAN
24-JUN-10	19:30 BST	CAPE TOWN	CAMEROON		NETHERLANDS

GROUP F

Date	Time	Venue	Team 1		Team 2
14-JUN-10	19:30 BST	CAPE TOWN	ITALY		PARAGUAY
15-JUN-10	12:30 BST	RUSTENBURG	NEW ZEALAND		SLOVAKIA
20-JUN-10	12:30 BST	BLOEMFONTEIN	SLOVAKIA		PARAGUAY
20-JUN-10	15:00 BST	NELSPRUIT	ITALY		NEW ZEALAND
24-JUN-10	15:00 BST	JOHANNESBURG (JEP)	SLOVAKIA		ITALY
24-JUN-10	15:00 BST	POLOKWANE	PARAGUAY		NEW ZEALAND

GROUP G

Date	Time	Venue	Team 1		Team 2
15-JUN-10	15:00 BST	PORT ELIZABETH	IVORY COAST		PORTUGAL
15-JUN-10	19:30 BST	JOHANNESBURG (JEP)	BRAZIL		NORTH KOREA
20-JUN-10	19:30 BST	JOHANNESBURG (JSC)	BRAZIL		IVORY COAST
21-JUN-10	12:30 BST	CAPE TOWN	PORTUGAL		NORTH KOREA
25-JUN-10	15:00 BST	DURBAN	PORTUGAL		BRAZIL
25-JUN-10	15:00 BST	NELSPRUIT	NORTH KOREA		IVORY COAST

GROUP H

Date	Time	Venue	Team 1		Team 2
16-JUN-10	12:30 BST	NELSPRUIT	HONDURAS		CHILE
16-JUN-10	15:00 BST	DURBAN	SPAIN		SWITZERLAND
21-JUN-10	15:00 BST	PORT ELIZABETH	CHILE		SWITZERLAND
21-JUN-10	19:30 BST	JOHANNESBURG (JEP)	SPAIN		HONDURAS
25-JUN-10	19:30 BST	PRETORIA	CHILE		SPAIN
25-JUN-10	19:30 BST	BLOEMFONTEIN	SWITZERLAND		HONDURAS

QUARTER-FINALS

	Date	Time	Venue		
(C) 5	2-JUL-10	15:00 BST	PORT ELIZABETH		7
(A) 1	2-JUL-10	19:30 BST	JOHANNESBURG (JSC)		3
(B) 2	3-JUL-10	15:00 BST	CAPE TOWN		4
(D) 6	3-JUL-10	19:30 BST	JOHANNESBURG (JEP)		8

SEMI-FINALS

	Date	Time	Venue		
(I) A	6-JUL-10	19:30 BST	CAPE TOWN		C
(II) B	7-JUL-10	19:30 BST	DURBAN		D

THIRD PLACE

	Date	Time	Venue		
LI	10-JUL-10	19:30 BST	PORT ELIZABETH		LII

FINAL

	Date	Time	Venue	
WI	11-JUL-10	19:30 BST	JOHANNESBURG (JSC)	WII

"In soccer everything is complicated by the presence of the opposite team."

JEAN PAUL SARTRE

WORLD CUP 2010 TEAMS

SOUTH AFRICA

The pessimists among South Africa supporters are relieved their country is staging the 2010 finals. It means, as hosts, their crisis-hit national team that they feared may not have been good enough to qualify, are automatically in the draw.

Despite all the fervour these first-ever African-staged finals is generating, the fortunes of the continent's host have plummeted.

After finishing a very creditable fourth when hosting the Confederations Cup in June 2009, the South African national side nicknmamed "Bafana Bafana" then embarked on a losing streak of eight out of their next nine games including 1-0 friendly defeats in Norway and Iceland.

This has added fuel to the controversy over the national coaching role. The South African FA (SAFA) sacked Joel Santana, then re-appointed Brazil's 1994 World Cup-winning coach, Carlos Alberto Parreira.

This decision had raised eyebrows as Parreira had taken charge in 2007, only to quit and return to Brazil when his wife was diagnosed with cancer.

However sympathetic to his wife's plight they were, some critics doubted Parreira's commitment. Many others wanted a successful local coach but the credentials of Jomo Sono, Clive Barker and

Gavin Hunt, who already had advisory roles in the SAFA, were disregarded.

SAFA president Kirsten Nematandani attempted to placate the growing number of critics by claiming Parreira would bring continuity as the squad was the one he had assembled originally and that he should be allowed to see through the process of the World Cup finals.

Parreira admits confidence had dropped to a very low level and said building morale was his primary task before the summer finals kick off.

The decline started in the closing stages of the Confederations Cup. They lost 1-0 to eventual-winners Brazil in the semi-finals, then an extra-time winner by European champions Spain robbed them of a third placing by 3-2.

Santana's optimistic talk of a "promising future" suddenly looked like pie in the sky as South Africa went into their worst run since they re-entered international soccer in 1992. Captain and centre back Aaron Mokoena said it had been

STAR PLAYER

STEVEN PIENAAR
Born: March 17, 1982 • **Club:** Everton (England)

A midfielder of massive energy, combined with an eye for a pass Pienaar's versatility is proven by his club Everton's use of him on the left while his country tends to prefer him in a more central role. Pienaar grew up in the township of Westbury and honed his skills at a local centre of excellence. He was spotted by scouts from Ajax Capetown, a feeder club for the famous Dutch club, and he ultimately went to Holland where he won league title medals with Ajax in 2002 and 2004. After an unhappy spell at Dortmund in Germany he revived his career with Everton. He says playing for South Africa at Johannesburg's new Soccer City will be a dream come true for him as it is close to his mother's home.

ONES TO WATCH

BERNARD PARKER
Born: March 16, 1986 • **Club:** FC Twente (Netherlands)

Parker is a pacy attacker who can play wide or through the middle. He netted both goals against New Zealand in South Africa's 2-0 Confederations Cup win and was named Man of the Match. Regular soccer in Europe has added to his sharpness.

MATTHEW BOOTH
Born: March 14, 1977 • **Club:** Mamelodi Sundowns (South Africa)

A real favourite with South African fans, it often sounds as though this 1.98m centre back is being booed whereas they are really chanting the name "Booth". The only white player to be a regular starter for South Africa, he inspires confidence with his solid performances. Booth plays his club soccer in South Africa now but although he made his international debut in 1999 his appearances were restricted by club commitments during seven years of playing in Russia.

difficult for the players to take so many defeats in succession. He added that being measured against the successes of previous squads increased the fear factor.

The Bafana Bafana have had a measure of success in the past 14 years. They won the African Cup of Nations in 1996, were runners-up two years later and finished third in 2000. They also reached the World Cup finals in 1998 and 2002. Then came a fallow period with a failure to qualify for the 2006 World Cup finals and elimination at the group stage of the 2008 African Nations Cup.

From among the successful old guard, captain Lucas Radebe retired and others such as Sibusiso Zuma and all-time record goalscorer Benni McCarthy were dropped from Santana's plans. Mokoena and midfielder Macbeth Sibaya are the only survivors from some of the previous successes.

Now Parreira is rebuilding confidence and expectations and in ex-Blackburn Rovers defender Mokoena, heading towards 100 caps, and centre-back partner Matthew Booth he has a bedrock of experience in defence. Also internationally-hardened are Sibaya, Maccabi Haifa attacker Thembinkosi Fanteni and fellow striker Bernard Parker who has seen service with Red Star Belgrade and FC Twente.

For invention Parreira will look to Everton midfielder Steven Pienaar who has consistently shown skill and industry in the English Premier League. The expectation is for Pienaar to lift players around him.

A desperate need is for a prolific striker as Parker and Katlego Mphela have not scored consistently and the statistics tell the sorry tale – South Africa's average is less than a goal a game in recent internationals. With goals crucial to South Africa's prospects of ending their crisis of confidence, McCarthy may yet emerge from the international wilderness.

MAN IN CHARGE

CARLOS ALBERTO PARREIRA

Globe-trotting Parreira's greatest achievement has been leading Brazil to World Cup victory in 1994 but he refused to return there as coach until 2006 where they lost 1-0 to France at the quarter-final stage. His coaching career with South Africa is also chequered as he took charge in 2007, quit within a short time, then was invited back to replace Joel Santana when Bafana Bafana was plunged into crisis. With South Africa he is heading for a record sixth World Cup finals as a coach after managing Kuwait in 1982, the United Arab Emirates in 1990 and Saudi Arabia in 1998. Never a professional player himself, Parreira took his first club coaching job in his native Brazil in 1967 and later took Fluminense to the Brazilian championship in 1984.

MEXICO

Mexico changed coaches in the middle of their qualification bid and recovered from potential disaster to reach South Africa on the back of a confident unbeaten six-game run.

Mexico's performances changed after Javier Aguirre took up his second spell as national coach to replace sacked former England boss Sven-Goran Eriksson.

Mexico have been World Cup finals fixtures since the competition's inception having only four times, since 1930, either not qualified or not entered. The present squad looked for a while as if they would break the chain and be only the fifth to fail to reach the finals.

Aguirre immediately began to re-energize the squad but did not make the best of starts with an embarrassing defeat in El Salvador in his first game in charge.

In the earlier 3rd round groups in the CONCACAF region, Mexico had qualified second to Honduras, then struggled at the start of the all-important 4th round stage. They had gathered just three points after four matches and suffered defeats in the United States and Honduras.

Under the new Aguirre era the Azteca stadium in Mexico City proved an inspiring venue for "El Tri" and they won all five games there plus a vital away 3-0 win over Costa Rica to qualify a point behind group winners USA.

Justifying the Eriksson sacking in mid-campaign, Mexican FA president Justino Compean said the decision was made because it was felt Mexico's participation in the World Cup finals was seriously at risk. Four days after going down 2-1 in El Salvador Aguirre's experimental side turned the corner to beat Trinidad and Tobago 2-1 – lift-off was achieved.

Veteran forward Cuauhtemoc Blanco, who played at France 98, said the win over Trinidad began to convince players and fans alike that Mexico would now go to the finals.

Then Miguel Sabah stepped into the hero's role when he came off the substitute's bench to hit the "most important goal of my career" – the 82nd-minute goal which beat the USA 2-1.

Then Mexico were South Africa-bound with a 3-0 away win which destroyed Costa Rica's 2010 ambitions. This was Giovani's game as he struck a

STAR PLAYER

RAFAEL MARQUEZ
Born: February 13, 1979 • **Club:** Barcelona (Spain)

Mexico rely on their captain Marquez for the experience he has accrued playing in European leagues and is the only Mexican to have won a European Champions' League winner's medal. He was in Barcelona's win over Arsenal in 2006 but injury prevented him from repeating that feat in Barcelona's 2009 victory over Manchester United. Marquez joined Barcelona from Monaco in 2003 and, although at club level he plays as centre back or defensive midfielder, Mexico prefer him in defence where he is commanding in the air and an inspirational figure. As a strong, determined and powerful "rock" for Mexico he has already won more than 80 caps. As a captain who leads by example he has even found the time to score 10 goals for his country.

GUILLERMO OCHOA

Born: July 13, 1985 • **Club:** America (Mexico)

Club scouts from around the world will be running the rule over Mexico's agile goalkeeper in South Africa. At just 25 he is already an experienced international with more than 30 caps. He made his club debut at 18 and was called into the national squad at 20. His assured handling made him one of the stars of Mexico's miserly defence in the unbeaten run to qualification.

RICARDO OSORIO

Born: March 30, 1980 • **Club:** Stuttgart (Germany)

His appearances in the 2006 World Cup in Germany were a springboard for Osorio's career. He was one of the stars of the Mexico side which reached the last 16 then was snapped up by German club Stuttgart for £3m after the finals. He helped them win the league title in his first season.

spectacular 30-yard goal then provided the assists for Franco and Andrés Guardado.

An all-round excellent team performance – solid at the back and sharp in attack – also demonstrated the new positive spirit engendered by Aguirre. They followed up with the home wins over Honduras and El Salvador which clinched Mexico's place in the upcoming South Africa draw with a game to spare.

Aguirre was backed to the hilt by his experienced players. Captain Rafael Marquez and defensive colleagues Carlos Salcido and Ricardo Osorio were regular choices with midfielders Gerrardo Torrado and Israel Castro.

Aguirre also blended players from Mexico's successful youth squads. Goalkeeper Guillermo Ochoa; defenders Efrain Juarez and Hector Moreno; midfielders Giovani, Andrés Guardado and Pablo Barrera; and strikers Carlos Vela, Omar Arellano and Enrique got a chance to show their mettle at a time when their country needed them. They all responded positively and Esqueda scored in Mexico's final 2-2 draw in Trinidad.

Aguirre said among the things he set out to correct was the defensive mistakes which had dogged the early part of the campaign and that he felt a great sense of satisfaction that he achieved that and booked Mexico's 14th appearance in the finals. They have not failed to qualify since 1990 when they were suspended by FIFA for fielding an over-age player in a youth tournament.

Only when Mexico had been hosts in 1970 and 1986 did they to advance to the quarter-finals. Their hopes were ended with a 4-1 hammering by Italy and a penalty shoot-out defeat by West Germany respectively.

Critics point to Mexico's vulnerability in the air if rock-steady Marquez is not around to deal with the high balls. They also question if the current midfield is dominant or the strikers will take enough chances to see Mexico advance to at least the quarter-finals again. Blanco was their top scorer in qualifying with three goals but two of these were penalties. Among the young guns, Aguirre will be looking to US-based Esqueda – or Arsenal's Vela for goals.

MAN IN CHARGE

JAVIER AGUIRRE

His second spell as Mexico coach was very much a firefighting job. The man who guided them to the last 16 in 2002 proved he had the ability to turn the national team around and get them winning again. In his first time around he had similarly come in to replace Enrique Meza in 2001 after a run of poor results. Under his guidance Mexico were 2001 Copa America finalists in addition to clinching World Cup qualification. He has bitter memories of being in the World Cup finals as a player. As an attacking midfielder he was one of the stars of the side which reached the quarter finals in 1986 but was sent off against West Germany before Mexico lost a penalty shoot-out.

URUGUAY

Despite two championships and two World Cup semi-final appearances, Uruguay cannot shake off the dominance of South American rivals Brazil and Argentina. After reaching South Africa via a play-off they need a convincing 2010 finals.

The winners of the first World Cup tournament in 1930 and again 20 years later are relying on attack this time to restore pride and the men they are looking to carry it through are Luis Suarez and Diego Forlan.

Uruguay reached South Africa via a 2-1 aggregate play-off win over Costa Rica – the third consecutive time they have squeezed in that way. Losing 1-0 to Argentina earlier had wasted the chance of automatic 2010 qualification.

Centre back Diego Lugano was the play-off hero as he forced home the only goal in San Jose and gave Uruguay a platform to hold on for a 1-1 draw in Montevideo.

Suarez and Forlan have been on sparkling form and shared 12 goals in the qualifiers. They have also been on form for their clubs and Forlan, despite a disappointing time at Manchester United in England several years ago, led Uruguay's scorers with seven goals, including the winner away against Ecuador.

Manchester United fans never saw the best of Forlan, but he has proved himself at top level, for his country and in Spain's La Liga.

Brazil and Argentina continue to dominate South American soccer because Uruguay lack their big populations and resources to bring young players through. Local rivals, such as Chile and Paraguay, have also gained in strength and as a result competition to be the South American representatives at World Cup finals has become more intense.

When Uruguay won its two World Cup championships, only 13 teams contested the finals. Their stars such as Juan Schiaffino, Alcides Ghiggia, who scored the 1950 World Cup winner, Jose Santamaria and Roque Maspoli all developed in their homeland. Now, promising youngsters such as Suarez move abroad as teenagers.

Coach Oscar Tabarez has the job of harnessing some prodigious young talent to the national cause in South Africa but admits that the lack of

STAR PLAYER

LUIS SUAREZ
Born: January 24, 1987 • **Club:** Ajax (Netherlands)

Striker Suarez forms Uruguay's striking spearhead alongside Diego Forlan. His versatility in operating through the centre or coming in from the wing has made him the rising star of Uruguayan soccer. His scoring feats – including netting five goals in Uruguay's World Cup qualifiers, have already made him a target for the top clubs in England and Spain. As a teenager Suarez helped Nacional win the Uruguayan title before leaving for FC Groningen in the Netherlands in 2006. Ajax signed him for £6m in 2007. His Uruguay debut in 2007 was less auspicious as he was sent off for dissent against Colombia. He has since worked hard to improve his disciplinary record.

DIEGO FORLAN

Born: May 19, 1979 • **Club:** Atletico Madrid (Spain)

The 2009 Golden Shoe winner as Europe's top scorer will be under the spotlight in South Africa. Playing for Uruguay is a real family affair as Forlan's father, Pablo, played for his country at the 1974 finals. A prolific scorer in Spanish soccer with Atletico Madrid and twice finishing top scorer, Forlan Jnr has won more than 60 caps and netted more than 20 goals since his international debut in 2002.

CRISTIAN RODRIGUEZ

Born: September 30, 1985 • **Club:** Porto (Portugal)

Although he was offered a university place to study architecture, Rodriquez opted to build a soccer career instead with the Penarol club. The tricky left winger's talent was spotted early and by the age of 18 he was selected for Uruguay for whom he is one of the main suppliers of goal opportunities for strikers Suarez and Forlan. With more than 30 caps, he has gained a fiery reputation and picked up a number of cards in the qualifiers.

stability in the domestic game makes qualifying campaigns a "traumatic experience."

Uruguay's 2010 qualification campaign included a 3-1 home win over Colombia and a 2-1 away victory over Ecuador to put the team's destiny in their own hands against Argentina.

Tabarez has a strong core of European-based stars including Gondin, Lugano, Perez, Suarez, Forlan, defenders Martin Caceres and Maxi Pereira and midfielders Sebastian Eguren and Walter Gargano. Winger Cristian Rodriguez and veteran back-up striker Sebastian Abreu are also part of the foreign legion. Tabarez needs them all to stay fit in their respective 2009-10 league programmes so that he has them available in South Africa. He also needs them to steer clear of red and yellow cards.

Tabarez was in charge when Uruguay reached the last 16 at Italia 90, only to lose 2-0 to the home nation. It was the only time since 1970 they have advanced beyond the group stage. Uruguay, despite their excellent World Cup pedigree failed to qualify in 1978, 1982, 1994, 1998 or 2006 and in the latter they lost a play-off penalty shoot-out to Australia.

Ironically, Uruguay had beaten the Australians 3-1 on aggregate to make their last finals appearance in 2002. Once there they lost their opening game 2-1 to Denmark, then drew 0-0 with France. They staged a thrilling comeback to draw 3-3 with quarter-finalists Senegal, but went home early.

Uruguayan fans will be pinning their hopes on Suarez and Forlan but they know deep down that if their team, nicknamed La Celeste, survive the group stage, it will be a major achievement.

MAN IN CHARGE

OSCAR TABAREZ

Having returned to take charge of the national side in 2006 after a 16-year absence, the man who saw Uruguay through to the last 16 of Italia 90 has steered them to the finals again. Tabarez, nicknamed "The Professor" for his thoughtful approach to coaching and strategy, had also guided Uruguay's leading club Penarol to Copa Libertadores victory in 1987. He left his last club job, at Boca Juniors in Argentina, in 2002 to become a TV analyst. After Uruguay failed to qualify for the 2006 finals in Germany he took them to the Copa America semi-finals in 2007 where they lost to eventual-winners Brazil in a penalty shoot-out.

FRANCE

France has the added burden of restoring their reputation by overcoming the controversy of qualifying through Thierry Henry's double handball. They must also find cohesion and prove they are not just a group of talented individuals.

The cheating row has seriously tarnished the 1998 world champions and 2006 World Cup finalists and eccentric coach Raymond Domenech has work to do to put a shine back on France's game after an erratic qualifying campaign.

The talented team rarely reached their potential in qualifying and ultimately left themselves a point behind group winners Serbia before they needed a dubious goal, via Henry's hand, to advance via the play-offs at the Republic of Ireland's expense.

Protests and tumultuous calls for replays were rejected and despite Henry owning up to twice handling before passing to goalscorer William Gallas it controversially stood. The goal gave France a draw on the night and a 2-1 aggregate win.

Domenech's relationship with the French sporting press and public has been rocky at times and there have been calls for the amateur astrologer to be fired but the French Football Federation has kept faith in him. It is shades of previous coach Aime Jacquet who was much criticised but steered France to their first-ever World Cup victory in 1998 then quit leaving a chastened but grateful nation saying "sorry."

The prophets of doom in the media fear a South African re-run of the French nightmare under Jacquet's successor, Roger Lemerre, in 2002. France were eliminated at the group stage without scoring a goal, after losing to Senegal and Denmark and drawing with Uruguay. Yet Domenech must take the credit for France's appearance in the 2006 final. He persuaded the great midfielder Zinedine Zidane, defender Lilian Thuram and midfield anchor Claude Makelele to come out of international retirement and he nurtured stars such as Henry and Franck Ribery.

There was controversy for Domenech again, this time in the final against Italy where so much hung on Zidane headbutting Italy's Materazzi in an off-the-ball incident and ending his career in the shame of a sending off. Even after France's ignominious exit from Euro 2008, Domenech stayed despite a national outcry.

France go to South Africa with a very talented squad. Hugo Lloris is an outstanding young

STAR MAN

THIERRY HENRY
Born: August 17, 1977 • **Club:** Barcelona (Spain)

Henry's record of more than 100 caps and being his country's all-time record scorer with more than 50 goals, speaks for how good a servant he has been to his country. France's Player of the Year in 2000, 2003, 2004, 2005 and 2006, he made his France debut in October 1997 and had reached 100 caps by June 2008. His World Cup finals scoring record is also impressive. He netted three times at France 98, but was an unused substitute for the final victory over Brazil. He was also one of the stars of France's Euro 2000 success, scoring three goals but was sent off against Uruguay as France were eliminated at the group stage of the 2002 World Cup finals. He also netted three times in the 2006 finals, including the vital quarter-final winner against Brazil.

ONES TO WATCH

YOANN GOURCUFF

Born: July 11, 1986 • **Club:** Bordeaux

As France's current Player of the Year, attacking midfielder Gourcuff is being predicted to be the man to step into the much-missed boots of the great Zinedine Zidane. Gourcuff has become France's creative spark but proved he can also play as a support striker with a spectacular 30-yard shot for his first international goal. Injuries cut short his Italian career with AC Milan but, now with Bordeaux, he starred in their 2009 league title victory.

HUGO LLORIS

Born: December 26, 1986 • **Club:** Lyon

Goalkeeper Lloris has roared on to the international scene for France after establishing himself as Nice's No1 goalkeeper at the age of 20. He has been called France's find of the qualifying campaign for his outstanding performances. He made his competitive international debut in the home qualifier against Romania and was outstanding in both games against the Republic of Ireland. His predecessor for club and country, Gregory Coupet, describes him as a "phenomenon".

goalkeeper, defender William Gallas offers experience and Patrice Evra is one of the world's top left backs. Defensive midfield duties are for Lassana Diarra and Yoann Gourcuff is being touted as the heir to Zidane. The attacking force includes Henry, Nicolas Anelka and Karim Benzema while winger Ribery is their supply line.

With that sort of talented line-up to call upon, it is a mystery why France struggled through qualifying. They opened with a shock 3-1 defeat in Austria but Henry and Anelka scored in a 2-1 win over the Serbs in Paris. Ribery and Gourcuff rescued a point after France trailed 2-0 in Romania after 16 minutes.

More dropped points with a draw against the Romanians in Paris meant France needed to win in Belgrade. Henry's goal cancelled out Nenad Milijas's early penalty then Lloris was sent off for an alleged trip on Serbia striker Nikola Zigic. The French were aggrieved because TV replays suggested the keeper barely made contact with the player.

Injuries to Ribery and Barcelona defender Eric Abidal did not help the French cause, neither did France's vulnerability in the air with Abidal, Escude and Sebastien Squillaci all failing to convince against aerial bombardment.

Press and public continued to query Domenech's decision to employ two defensive midfielders in Lassana Diarra and Jeremy Toulalan or Alou Diarra and, in attack, the choice of Andre-Pierre Gignac for the closing games, ahead of Benzema and Florent Malouda.

In the opening play-off tie against Ireland in Dublin, Anelka's deflected shot gave them the lead but Robbie Keane's goal at the Stade de France set nerves jangling. Next came the shoddy incident that sent France to South Africa and, given the controversy that followed, the French might regret the damage to their reputation for fair play. Henry blatantly took the ball out of the air with his hand, handled a second time, and crossed for Gallas to head France's extra-time winner.

49

MAN IN CHARGE

RAYMOND DOMENECH

Domenech is one of the coaches who will be most under pressure. Unpopular with the press and public in France, he probably needs a top four finish in South Africa to placate his critics. But he did take France to the 2006 World Cup final where they lost to Italy on penalties. Domenech was promoted from national under-21 coach to succeed Jacques Santini after France's disappointing performance at Euro 2004 but there was a clamour for his sacking after France were eliminated at the group stage of Euro 2008. He was constantly under pressure from media and fans throughout the 2010 qualifying campaign as France trailed Serbia. The manner of France's ultimate qualification via the Henry double handball cannot have helped.

ARGENTINA

Just for a while in the qualifying period for South Africa 2010, the unthinkable – no Argentina in the finals – looked on the cards. But with Diego Maradona at the helm, and not as a player, the "White and Sky Blues" will be there

Argentina had been in danger of failing to reach the finals for the first time since 1970 before Mario Bolatti's winner against Uruguay earned a reprieve. The final South American group game was a must-win scenario for Argentina and their rivals, and neighbours, Uruguay.

The winner would go to South Africa; the defeated faced a play-off where another threat of elimination loomed.

Bolatti sent his country and their controversial coach Diego Maradona back to the World Cup finals where they had twice gone on to be champions in 1974 and 1886.

But being this close to qualifying elimination is not what they envisaged after six games of Maradona's reign as coach. He had been a great, if erratic, servant to Argentina as a brilliant No 10 but was untried as a coach, except for a short time at club level.

Argentina's soccer bosses chose Maradona to succeed Alfio Basile in November 2008. Basile had steered Argentina to the 2007 Copa America final but quit after a first competitive defeat to Chile, a 1-0 loss in Santiago. Qualifying still looked on the cards as Argentina held the third automatic qualifying place with eight games left, ahead of Chile on goal difference. Although Sergio Daniel Batista, who had led Argentina's Under-23 squad to Olympic gold in Beijing weeks before, seemed the obvious choice to succeed Basile, Maradona, controversial as ever, threw his hat into the ring.

Noray Nakis, head of the selection committee, backed Maradona's candidature and Argentine Football Association president Julio Grondona confirmed him in the job. But the question on the soccer public's lips was: did Maradona have star quality as a coach as well?

Undoubtedly he had been Argentina's greatest-ever player, but his last coaching job had been at Buenos Aires side Racing Club, which ended in 1995.

Critics warned that appointing a playing legend had not always worked before although supporters of Maradona cited West Germany's triumphant captain of 1974, Franz Beckenbauer, steering

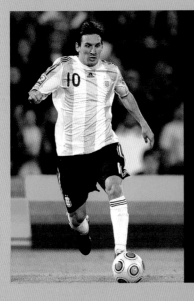

STAR PLAYER

LIONEL MESSI
Born: June 24, 1987 • **Club:** Barcelona (Spain)

Argentina has the jewel of world soccer in the slightly-built, but lethal, Messi. He is currently regarded as the world's top player for his dribbling skill, acceleration and clinical finishing. For one so young, he has already tasted great success. He was one of the stars of Argentina's victory in the 2008 Olympic soccer tournament and was key to his club's 2009 European Champions league title and Spanish league and cup double success. Messi was not on his best form for Argentina's unconvincing 2010 qualifying campaign but he still scored four goals. At eight days short of his 19th birthday he got his first World Cup experience – as a substitute in Argentina's 6-0 win over Serbia and Montenegro at Germany 2006.

ONES TO WATCH

JAVIER MASCHERANO
Born: June 8, 1984 • **Club:** Liverpool (England)

Mascherano was made Argentina's captain after Diego Maradona took over as national coach and has won more than 50 caps for his country. As one of the world's top defensive midfield players, his role is to break up opponents' attacks. His consistent performances have made him a regular for Argentina since he made his international debut in 2001 after starring in the World Under-17 championship. He won gold at the Olympic soccer tournaments of 2004 and 2008.

SERGIO "KUN" AGUERO
Born: June 2, 1988 • **Club:** Atletico Madrid (Spain)

Another member of the Argentina side which won 2008 Olympic soccer gold, Aguero has been playing top-level soccer since he was 15. He was the youngest-ever player to appear in Argentina's top division when, at 15 years and 35 days, he made his debut for Independiente in 2003. He won his first Argentina cap later that same year.

them to the 1986 and 1990 World Cup finals and triumphing in the latter.

Maradona started by ousting veteran Javier Zanetti as captain and installing Javier Mascherano even though the Liverpool midfielder publicly doubted his own ability to do the job.

The coach then switched tactics to 3-4-3, using three small attackers, Lionel Messi, Carlos Tevez and Sergio Aguero but later reverted to 4-4-2.

Maradona chopped and changed his sides and eventually used 49 players in qualifying. He gave promising youngsters from the domestic league such as Nicolas Otamendi their international chance and recalled veterans Juan Veron and Martin Palermo but his side crashed humiliatingly 6-1 in Bolivia and lost 2-0 in Ecuador.

Argentina's place in South Africa came under serious threat after defeats by Brazil and Paraguay and the coach dismissed the gathering clamour to resign. Maradona responded by selecting internationally-inexperienced centre backs Sebastian Dominguez and Otamendi at home to Brazil but lost again 3-1. Brazilians Luisao and Luis Fabiano successfully exploited Argentina's vulnerability in dead-ball situations.

Maradona told his soccer-crazy nation not to panic but worse was

to follow. Argentina lost 1-0 in Paraguay with Veron was sent off. The scenario now being Argentina had to win their last two games to qualify automatically in fourth place.

There were sighs of relief across the country when Palermo scrambled a 92nd-minute winner against Peru and, six minutes from time, substitute Bolatti scored the only goal to thwart the Uruguayans' ambitions for the moment.

Based on their qualifying roller coaster Argentina, and Maradona, face a stiff task in the finals to maintain Argentina's proud record of two championships, two runners-up places and three quarter-finals as well as coming up with a team to please the fans.

51

MAN IN CHARGE

DIEGO MARADONA
Maradona needs no introduction as he was one of the greatest players of all time – but as a coach he is a rookie. He has thrust himself into the full glare of the limelight as national coach when his only previous coaching experience lasted barely a year at club level in the 1990s. His attacking genius inspired Argentina to World Cup victory in 1986 and his second goal in the 1986 quarter final against England was voted "Goal of the Century" in a 2002 FIFA poll. Ever controversial, Maradona was sent home from the 1994 World Cup finals after testing positive for the stimulant ephedrine.

NIGERIA

Expectations will be high for the new generation of Nigeria's "Super Eagles" in South Africa. After failing in the quarter finals of the 2008 African Cup of Nations, Nigeria looked set to disappoint again in qualification for South Africa.

In short, it was touch and go for a while whether talent-packed Nigeria would be making the relatively-short trip south to the 2010 World Cup finals. They came perilously close to an early exit and the fact they staved off World Cup disaster was greeted with relief rather than triumph.

It was an inspired substitution which dragged Nigeria back from the brink of an unexpected defeat in Kenya. Obafemi Martins came off the bench to score twice in Nigeria's 3-2 win.

Previous group leaders Tunisia lost 1-0 in Mozambique allowing Nigeria to top their African group by a single, but decisive, point.

Since their first World Cup finals' qualification and subsequent advancement to the second round in 1994, Nigeria's soccer-loving public expects its "Super Eagles" to soar on the big stages.

Before the Kenya game it looked as though the unthinkable was happening – a second consecutive failure to qualify after not making it to Germany in 2006.

First Dario's 83rd-minute winner for Mozambique threw the Nigerians a lifeline they had to grasp; then their coach Shaibu Amodu made an inspired substitution. With his side trailing 1-0 in Nairobi, he sent on Martins as a twin spearhead alongside Yakubu Aiyegbeni – and it worked. Martins levelled, Yakubu added a second – and Martins grabbed the winner.

Former skipper Nwankwo Kanu remembered how upsetting it had been watching other African teams steal the show in Germany and he said Nigeria couldn't afford another experience like that.

It had looked as though Amodu's fourth spell as national coach might be under threat with Tunisia's last-gasp equaliser in a 2-2 draw in Abuja. Nigeria needed two wins from their last two games and, more crucially, Martins and Yakubu back from injury.

The need to unify in order to qualify was disrupted by a row between the coach and senior players over the omission of winger John Utaka.

STAR PLAYER

OBAFEMI MARTINS
Born: October 28, 1984 • **Club:** Wolfsburg (Germany)

Often celebrating with a trademark somersault, Nigeria's most prolific striker has averaged more than a goal every other game since his debut in 2004. Small, quick and effervescent Martins is a predator in the penalty box. He was Africa's Young Player of the Year in 2003 and 2004 and has his sights on Yekini's national record of 37 goals for Nigeria. Having played for top-level clubs in Italy, Germany and England, he brings huge experience to the national team. He joined Reggiana from Nigerian side Ebedei in 2000 and has furthered his career with Internazionale, Newcastle United and Wolfsburg.

ONES TO WATCH

JOSEPH YOBO
Born: September 6, 1980 • **Club:** Everton (England)

With his defensive organisation and calming influence centre back Yobo has taken over from Kanu as Nigeria's skipper. His strength in the air, consistency and vast experience of pressure games make him one of the first names on the Nigeria team sheet and he has gained more than 60 caps. He appeared in all three of Nigeria's games at the 2002 finals.

MIKEL JOHN OBI
Born: April 22, 1987 • **Club:** Chelsea (England)

Being the subject of a bitter transfer battle in 2006 between two of England's Premiership giants, Manchester United and Chelsea, is a testament to Mikel's worth. He finally opted for Chelsea for a £16m fee – a far cry from when the forceful midfield anchor Mikel joined Ajax's South African offshoot from Nigerian club Plateau United. Mikel was one of Nigeria's stars when they reached the World Under-20 Championship final in 2005 and has played more than 20 full internationals for Nigeria.

Despite calls for Amodu's sacking, the Nigerian Football Association stuck by him saying it was not the time for panic measures. Nigeria's World Cup finals' record is as good as almost any of their African rivals. They reached the last 16 at France 98, but lost 4-1 to Denmark.

Four years later, they were unfortunate enough to be drawn into a "Group of Death" and were eliminated as England and Sweden went on. Nigeria's only consolation was that the other team in that group – the mighty Argentina – also went home early.

Nigeria's best World Cup performance came on their first appearance, in 1994. Buoyed by a number of stars who were making their names in Europe, the "Super Eagles" entered the US-staged finals as African champions. Their side included record scorer Rashidi Yekini, midfield general Jay-Jay Okocha and Sunday Oliseh. They led eventual-finalists Italy 1-0 through Amunike's goal until the 88th minute of their last 16 clash before Roberto Baggio equalised then hit an extra-time winner from the penalty spot.

For 2010 Amodu can call upon an array of stars doing well in European leagues. He has Wolfsburg's Martins, Yakubu of Everton, Lokomotiv Moscow striker Peter Odemwingie and Malaga's Obinna to offer attacking thrust.

Joseph Yobo has been a reliable mainstay of the Everton defence in the English Premiership for four seasons and in the national side has built a solid partnership with Sion centre back Obinna Nwaneri. Chelsea's John Obi Mikel is the shield for the back four while Seye Olifinjana adds midfield industry.

Since the retirement of Okocha, Nigeria have lacked a playmaker and Amodu will be hoping a suitable player for the role presents itself before the first kick of the finals in summer 2010.

53

MAN IN CHARGE

SHAIBU AMODU

Amodu just cannot turn down the call of his country and in his fourth spell as Nigeria coach. But he has yet to take a team through a World Cup finals stage. He first took charge of the national team after the 1994 World Cup, when he succeeded Clemens Westerhof for a year. He stepped in again before Philippe Troussier arrived to lead Nigeria at France 98. In his third spell, he guided them to the 2002 World Cup finals, but was replaced by Adegboye Onigbinde for the tournament. Amodu took over again in April 2008. Earlier in his career he had been successful with a number of African club sides but many fans would prefer a more high-profile coach to lead their national team.

SOUTH KOREA

South Korea's 2010 quest as the most successful Asian side in World Cup history is to continue proving it. In their seventh World Cup finals they will be looking to beat their surprise 4th place in 2002.

South Korea have already shown their good form by comfortably easing through Asia's so-called "Group of Death" and for coach Huh Jung-Moo the question now is can his side team emulate their illustrious predecessors of 2002 and reach the semi-finals again?

South Korea remain the only Asian team ever to reach the last four but they were on home territory and benefited from fervent crowd support as co-hosts with Japan.

The more-disingenuous observers say contentious decisions went South Korea's way against Italy in the last 16 and then against Spain in the quarter-finals before their ultimate 1-0 defeat to Germany.

There are no doubts that, historically, they have struggled in World Cup finals staged outside their home region. In those six instances they have not made it past the first round. As the Korea Republic in their first World Cup in 1954 they were humiliated in two group matches, 9-0 by Hungary and 7-0 against Turkey.

South Korea's high hopes for the Germany 2006 finals ended in their early elimination. They went home early after a 2-0 defeat by Switzerland, despite a win over Togo and a draw with France.

After two Dutch coaches of the national team – Guus Hiddink in charge in 2002 and Dick Advocaat four years later, home-grown coach Huh was a controversial choice when he was appointed in 2007 – his third spell as national coach.

He was given the twin responsibilities of qualifying for the 2010 World Cup finals while developing young players to revitalise the ageing squad inherited from 2006. The sniping at Huh did not stop even as South Korea eased through pre-qualifying with their bitter rivals and northern neighbours North Korea, from a group which included Jordan and Turkmenistan.

Huh was also criticised for lack of organisation and tactical nous when North Korea looked the better side in a 1-1 draw in the opening game of the final qualifiers which, because of political differences, had to be played in neutral Shanghai in China.

Huh hit back by pointing to the number of important players missing because of European

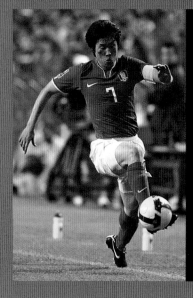

STAR PLAYER

PARK JI-SUNG
Born: February 25, 1981 • **Club:** Manchester United (England)

The all-action midfielder is undoubtedly one of the world's most famous Koreans as he has starred with, not only the national team, but also top clubs PSV Eindhoven and Manchester United. Despite already being a national hero in his country he may feel he has something to prove in South Africa, after the early elimination of the South Korea team of which he was a part at Germany 2006. Park's return, after missing the opening final-group qualifier for 2010 against North Korea, lifted the players around him. Huh has made him captain and he led by example and scored three times in the group. He is well on the way to gaining 100 caps for his country.

LEE PYONG-YO

Born: April 23, 1977 • **Club:** Al-Hilal (Saudi Arabia)

Although not a regular starter now the veteran left back is considered a valuable influence on his younger colleagues in the national team. His experience is second to none having played in European club soccer and being one of only seven South Koreans who have passed 100 caps. South Africa will be his third finals' appearance.

PARK CHU-YOUNG

Born: July 10, 1985 • **Club:** Monaco (France)

The once bright young hope of South Korean soccer has been blighted by injuries and inconsistency since he made his international debut as a teenager against Uzbekistan in 2005. There are now high hopes for him in South Africa if can find and maintain the excellent form he displayed in the qualifiers. The speedy winger can also play as a support striker and he scored twice in qualifying to inspire wins over Saudi Arabia and the UAE.

club commitments. Star midfielder Park Ji-Sung and veteran defender Lee Pyong-yo proved Huh's point by returning for the next game and inspiring South Korea to a 4-1 win over the United Arab Emirates. Park Ji-Sung even got himself on the score sheet.

The Koreans' 2-0 win in Saudi Arabia – aided by the dismissal of home player Naif Hazazi – was South Korea's first win over the Saudis for 19 years.

Park Ji-Sung was then on target again with an 81st-minute equaliser as South Korea drew 1-1 in Iran. In the next game substitute Kim Chi-Woo floated an 87th-minute free kick straight into North Korea's net for a 1-0 win. With only a win against the UAE needed to clinch their finals place, South Korea led 2-0 after 37 minutes and won at a stroll.

With the knowledge that the air tickets for South Africa were booked, Huh was able to experiment with his line-up and achieved home draws against Saudi Arabia and Iran and wins in friendlies with Paraguay and Australia.

Having transformed his squad, Huh was beginning to get more generous support from the South Korean Press for what he was achieving.

Goalkeeper Lee Woon-Jae, Lee Pyong-yo and defender Kim

Nam-Il are the only remnants of the old guard that Huh had inherited. Defender Oh Beomseok, midfielders Ki Sung-yeung, Lee Chung-yong and Park Chu-young and striker Lee Keun-ho represent Huh's younger generation. Manchester United's Park Ji-Sung – a leading three-goal scorer in qualifying with Lee Keun-ho – said he believes the team is coming together nicely in time for South Africa while Huh continues his search for a prolific striker and is hoping young Lee Keun-ho will step into that role.

MAN IN CHARGE

HUH JUNG-MOO

There were calls for a bigger name when Huh was appointed for his third spell as national coach in December 2007. He had just only managed a mid-table place for Chunnam Dragons in the K-League club soccer. Huh first took charge in 1995, then again from 1998 to 2000 when he was succeeded by Guus Hiddink. Huh shrugged off the criticism and succeeded in his task to guide South Korea to their seventh finals, while still rebuilding the squad. He not only beat off the challenge of bitter rivals North Korea but also with a run of four wins and a draw inspired the team through to South Africa with two matches to spare. Huh will be the third South Korean to go to the finals as both player and coach.

GREECE

Euro 2004 winners Greece go to South Africa hoping to improve on their only previous World Cup finals' appearance which ended at the first hurdle, but in long-serving coach Otto Rehhagel they have an inspirational leader.

Critics might say that a single goal by Dimitrios Salpingidis saved the job German-born Rehhagel has held since 2001. Questions were being asked about Greece's coach after their failure to qualify for the Germany World Cup of 2006 was followed by a catastrophic early exit from the finals of Euro 2008 which lost their European crown.

Salpingidis' winner was in a must-win play-off in Ukraine after Greece had finished second in European Group Two. On the way the Greeks had lost at home and away to automatic qualifiers Switzerland. This left Rehhagel under fire for allegedly outdated and over-cautious tactics, especially after he played five at the back in the 0-0 first leg draw against Ukraine in Athens.

His theory was that it was vital not to concede an away goal to Ukraine, who have lethal strikers such as Andriy Shevchenko to call up.

Most of all Rehhagel had the backing of his players in this view. Midfielder Kostas Katsouranis said a goalless home draw kept the team's hopes alive.

In the return Rehhagel used a 5-4-1 formation with two wide players, Salpingidis and Giorgios Samaras, breaking in support of striker Angelos Charisteas. After 31 minutes Salpingidis shot home and then it was up to two stalwart centre backs, Vangelis Moras and Sokratis Papasatathopoulos to hold out under pressure.

Rehhagel can withstand the pressure of critics. When he was later asked if he would ever play an attacking game, he joked that it would only be when he could field Argentina's Lionel Messi, Brazil's Kaka and Spain's Xavi and Andres Iniesta.

After a successful club career with Werder Bremen in Germany Rehhagel pulled off one of the biggest international shocks in steering unfancied Greece to victory at Euro 2004. Again the purists sneered at Greece's dogged defence and emphasis on dead-ball moves but they surprised France in the quarter-finals, the Czech Republic in the semis and hosts Portugal in the final – and without conceding a goal.

To the critics of his defensive approach Rehhagel

STAR PLAYER

THEOFANIS GEKAS
Born: May 23, 1980 • **Club:** Bayer Leverkusen (Germany)

This prolific scorer for Greece has averaged almost a goal every other game since his debut, against Albania in 2005. He also finished Europe's top scorer in 2010 qualifying with 10 goals. Although he has had a recent unsettled club career at Bayer Leverkusen in Germany and Portsmouth in England he says the Greek system of play is geared towards his game. His most important contributions for qualifying this time around came in the last two group games when he netted four times in Greece's 5-2 win over Latvia then scored the second goal in the 2-1 win over Luxembourg which clinched their play-off place.

ONES TO WATCH

ANGELOS CHARISTEAS

Born: February 9, 1980 • **Club:** Nurnberg (Germany)

The winner of more than 80 caps since scoring twice on his debut, against Russia in 2001, Charisteas then became the hero of Greece's Euro 2004 victory by heading the winning goal against Portugal in the final. He also scored against Spain and France and was named in the UEFA Team of the Tournament. At 6ft 3in tall his Greek colleagues have the ideal target man and he scored four goals in the qualifiers.

GIORGIOS KARAGOUNIS

Born: March 6, 1977 • **Club:** Panathinaikos (Greece)

Inspirational as Greece's elder statesman and captain, midfield playmaker and dead-ball expert, Karagounis is one of Greece's most successful soccer exports. He is also another of the Euro 2004 heroes for scoring the first goal of the tournament in a 2-1 group win over Portugal. He has won more than 90 caps since his debut in 1999 and clubwise he returned to Athens club Panathinaikos from Benfica in 2007.

says he makes the best use of the players available and points to his club career at Werder Bremen which nurtured attacking stars such as Rudi Voller and Karl-Heinz Riedle.

Switzerland's German boss Ottmar Hitzfeld also backs Rehhagel and rates him as "a very clever coach who adapts to circumstances."

Greece's strength is their defence because of an abundance of strong, physical players although they also have a penalty box poacher in Theofanis Gekas who finished top scorer in the European qualifiers with 10 goals.

Rehhagel is not relying on Greek players contracted to foreign clubs as his mainstay and has built the squad on a core of Panathinaikos stars. The club from the Greek capital of Athens is supplying goalkeeper Alexandros Tzorvas; full backs Nikos Spiropoulos and Lukas Vyntra; centre back Giorgios Setaridis; skipper Girogios Karagounis; Katsouranis; and Salpingidis to the national squad.

Goalkeeper Kostas Chalkias from PAOK and Olympiakos defender Vasilis Torsidis are other home-based players likely to figure in South Africa.

Blended into the squad with the home-grown stars are Greece's foreign legion – Moras with

Bologna; Papastathopoulos with Genoa; defender Sotirios Kyrgiakos who is in his first season at Liverpool and defensive midfielder Christos Pastazoglou turns out in Cyprus for Omonia Nicosia. Attackers Charisteas and Iannis Amanatidis play in Germany for Nurnberg and Eintracht Frankfurt respectively.

Greece's team have promised defensive grit and hard work to make up for the failure of the last time they reached the World Cup in the United States in 1994. Under Rehhagel they are united in trying to improve on their unenviable World Cup record of losing all their three group games without a goal being scored.

MAN IN CHARGE

OTTO REHHAGEL

At 71, Rehhagel will be making his first World Cup finals' appearance despite a long coaching career. Greece have not made it that far in the World Cup since he took charge in 2001. Rehhagel originally made his name at club level with Werder Bremen in the Bundesliga. He spent 14 years transforming them into one of Germany's top clubs and led them to two championships, two domestic cup successes and the European Cup Winners Cup. He also steered promoted Kaiserslautern to the Bundesliga title in 1998. Internationally his greatest triumph was guiding Greece to victory at Euro 2004 for which he was named Greek of the Year, the first foreigner to win the accolade.

ENGLAND

England is hungry to end a World Championship drought that has lasted 44 years. Their less-than-average record at world and European level since their 1966 World Cup triumph has put huge pressure on the current highly talented squad.

South Africa represents a test of the turn-around in England's fortunes under Italian coach Fabio Capello. Just two years after they failed to even qualify for Euro 2008, England are among the favourites for a 2010 triumph in South Africa.

Under Capello's unsmiling gaze, England have been transformed from a stuttering 2-0 win over Andorra in 2008 which was jeered by travelling fans to runaway winners in their European group from which a highly-rated Croatia failed to qualify.

On the way England crushed Croatia 5-1, who have had prevented England from qualifying for Euro 2008, to reach South Africa with two games to spare.

Their achievement of eight straight group wins and 31 goals scored has put England among the leading contenders for South Africa with the world's bookmakers.

The team's reaction to being booed in Andorra was astonishing as they went out four days later to heap their first dose of revenge on Croatia – a 4-1 away win.

Capello unleashed the pace of 19-year-old Theo Walcott, who scored a hat-trick in Croatia's first competitive home defeat. Capello has instilled discipline, self-belief and organization into his England squad and the goals have flowed. They scored three in the last 15 minutes to beat Kazakhstan 5-1 and defeated Belarus on their home turf 3-1.

Critics had consistently said that Chelsea's Frank Lampard and Liverpool's Steven Gerrard were too similar in style to play in tandem in England's midfield but Belarus was the game in which Capello solved the conundrum. Lampard played through central midfield and Gerrard started on the left to link with striker Wayne Rooney.

Gerrard says that under Capello England no longer play with fear and Lampard is enjoying the increasing confidence bursting through the team's performances.

Pivotal to Capello plans for England has been Manchester United man Rooney who has emerged the top scorer in qualification, as he revelled in his favourite role behind a powerful striker.

STAR PLAYER

WAYNE ROONEY
Born: October 24, 1985 • **Club:** Manchester United (England)

The dynamic Rooney has really blossomed as an attacking star under Capello's regime. He has emerged as England's biggest and consistent goal threat with nine goals in their opening eight qualifiers. He is powerful, pacy and capable of moments of brilliance – and petulance.

He operates as a second striker and has benefited from no longer playing second fiddle to Cristiano Ronaldo at Manchester United. He has a point to prove at major tournaments. He scored against Switzerland and Croatia at Euro 2004 before limping out of the quarter-final against Portugal. At Germany 2006 he was rushed back from a foot injury and used as a lone striker. His temperament let him down in England's quarter-final defeat by Portugal when he was sent off for a stamp on defender Ricardo Carvalho.

ONES TO WATCH

JOHN TERRY

Born: December 7, 1980 • **Club:** Chelsea (England)

Big John Terry is England's "Braveheart"; the man who leaps in where the boots are flying. The all-action captain loves laying himself on the line with block tackles or menacing opposition defences at set pieces. He remains Capello's leader on the pitch despite injuries taking their toll. The England stopper will be a physically-imposing defensive inspiration in South Africa.

STEVEN GERRARD

Born: May 30, 1980 • **Club:** Liverpool (England)

Gerrard was in for a surprise when Capello came in as the new England coach and changed the player's role. He seemed baffled at first to be used from the left but has since settled in the role and has been enjoying his most consistent spell for England specialising in spectacular goals, often blasted from outside the penalty box. Also good news for England fans is that he has developed an excellent understanding with Rooney.

ENGLAND v UKRAINE
Wednesday 1 April 2009, Wembley Stadium

Capello equates Rooney with the great Raul of Real Madrid and Spain in his influence on recent England performances. In defence, centre backs Terry and Rio Ferdinand have a great understanding and Ashley Cole is rated one of the world's finest left backs. Speed is an essential part of Capello's philosophy as proved by winger Aaron Lennon tearing apart Croatia's defence at Wembley and the timely inclusions in other games of fellow winger Walcott and striker Jermain Defoe as "impact" substitutes.

Injuries could scupper England's hopes with Ferdinand having an injury-prone 2009-10 domestic league campaign and central partner Terry a victim of recurrent back troubles. The coach will definitely want Rooney fully fit, unlike in Germany four years ago when he was rushed back into action, prematurely many felt, from a metatarsal fracture. Other problem areas of the team Capello has to ponder in the months before flying to South Africa are goalkeeper and a spearhead striker.

In goal he has experimented with Ben Foster, Robert Green, Joe Hart and the veteran David James but none have truly made themselves indispensable between the sticks. Enthusiastic attacking right back Glen Johnson of Liverpool is liable to be caught

out defensively and, although a powerful presence, Emile Heskey's scoring record for England and his club Aston Villa is poor. He notched just one goal during the qualifiers in the 4-0 win in Kazakhstan.

Capello's record suggests his squad is well equipped to peak in South Africa. But he is nothing if not a realist about World Cup finals in which he played for Italy in 1974. Despite being among the favourites, Capello and his Azzurri were eliminated at the group stage.

England will also be hoping for more than a World Cup 2010 triumph. Success on the pitch puts the country in the front of the shop window in their bid to host the 2018 finals.

MAN IN CHARGE

FABIO CAPELLO

"Iron Sergeant" Capello believes in discipline and non-stop concentration, so it is no accident that his teams often score late winners. As a single-minded coach he is not swayed by the media, players' reputations or, as in his AC Milan days, even Italian prime minister and club owner Silvio Berlusconi. Capello steered Milan to the European Cup in 1994 and four Italian titles then led Roma to their first championship for 17 years in 2000 before switching to Spain to guide Real Madrid to two Spanish league crowns. On paper he is one of the most-successful coaches in the world. He will only select those who are playing regularly and in form. That's why he has ignored the claims for injury-hit Michael Owen and advised David Beckham to go on loan at Milan outside the US season.

UNITED STATES

Never underestimate the United States (US) in World Cup competitions. Just ask the England team of 1950, the Brazil side of 2009 and Spain the top-ranked team of the 2010 finals.

The rapid development of grass-roots soccer in American football-dominated USA is now emerging at international level. In a preview of what might come in 2010, the US led Brazil 2-0 at half-time in the Confederations Cup final in South Africa last summer before eventually going down 3-2.

Strikes from Clint Dempsey and key man Landon Donovan gave them command inside 27 minutes against Brazil. This was not the first American shock in this competition. In the semi-finals they ended Spain's 35-game unbeaten run with a shock 2-0 win thanks to goals from Jozy Altidore and Clint Dempsey.

The US has a history of taking big-name scalps that should not be ignored in the World Cup finals in South Africa.

The unfancied Americans' 1-0 win over an all-powerful England in the 1950 finals, thanks to Larry Gaetjens's goal, remains firmly in World Cup folklore.

Memories of what might have been against Brazil still haunt the US players. They are disappointed with themselves that at 2-0 up, they should have been able to kill the game off. They now know that the one team you do not give second chances to is Brazil.

The results during the 2009 run-up to the South Africa World Cup, which will be the US' sixth visit to the finals, are proof to US coach Bob Bradley that the US players have raised their standards – and expectations. The national team is benefiting from having a well-organised major league at home and a diaspora of American players turning out for major European clubs.

Donovan has played for top Bundesliga sides Bayer Leverkusen and Bayern Munich; Tim Howard is Everton's first choice goalkeeper in the English Premier League and US skipper Carlos Bocanegra is with Rennes after four years in England. Midfielder Dempsey is a firm favourite at Fulham, while West Ham full back Jonathan Spector is another Premiership regular. Centre backs Oguchi

STAR PLAYER

LANDON DONOVAN

Born: March 4, 1982 • **Club:** Los Angeles Galaxy (United States)

Donovan is a record breaker for his country. He is the only American to have won more than 100 caps – South Africa will see him come close to 130 – and has scored more than 40 goals for his country, both records. At only 28 he is probably the most outstanding of all the US stars, a fact registered by his peers and public as in 2009 he was named Player of the Year for the sixth time in nine seasons plus given the additional accolade of Player of the Decade. Donovan was first capped as a 20-year-old and scored against Poland and Mexico during the Americans' run to the 2002 World Cup quarter-finals. Attacking midfielder/striker Donovan joined German club Bayer Leverkusen in 1999 but moved back to his native California with LA Galaxy in 2005.

ONES TO WATCH

JOZY ALTIDORE
Born: November 6, 1989 • **Club:** Hull City (England, loan)

Altidore is the most expensive player to come out of the MSL. The striker who made his debut for Red Bulls in the US as a 16-year-old moved to Villarreal in Spain in June 2008 for a fee of £7m. He led the US scorers in qualifying for South Africa with five goals, including a hat-trick against Trinidad and the winner at home to El Salvador. He also scored the opener in the Americans' Confederations Cup win over Spain.

CARLOS BOCANEGRA
Born: May 25, 1979 • **Club:** Rennes (France)

US captain Bocanegra is a powerful force at both ends of the pitch. He is a wily centre back who gets vital goals for his country such as his winner in the home qualifier against Honduras. Capped more than 70 times, he currently plays for Rennes in France after four seasons with Fulham in the English Premier League. He says he dreams of playing in Spain before his career is over.

Onyewu (Milan) and Steve Cherundolo (Hannover) have also established themselves in Europe.

The country's world ambitions are embodied in the continuing policy of blooding youngsters such as striker Altidore on the international scene and developing Major League Soccer (MLS) talent, like Houston Dynamos' Ricardo Clark and Chivas USA defender Jonathan Bornstein.

It has been a long time since anyone underestimated the Americans in soccer circles. They qualified in 1990, very successfully hosted the finals in 1994 and have qualified for every World Cup finals since.

Their World Cup pinnacle so far was in 2002, when they reached the quarter finals only to go out 1-0 to eventual runners-up Germany.

To qualify for the 2010 finals they topped the final CONCACAF group, one point ahead of Mexico. The qualification has highlighted their fighting spirit, coming from 2-0 down to draw 2-2 with Costa Rica and, earlier in the qualifiers, when a Frankie Hejduk 88th-minute strike secured a 2-2 draw in El Salvador. Two away wins effectively secured for the US their place in South Africa. Clark scored the only goal in Trinidad and Tobago, then Donovan sealed a 3-2 win in Honduras after two

Conor Casey goals. Coach Bradley isn't without his injury woes with keystone player Onyewu racing against time to make the finals after knee surgery and striker Charlie Davies suffering serious car crash injuries.

The players are highly motivated to get their best World Cup result yet and Bocanegra praises Bradley as a dynamic coach who inspires his players to approach games with the right mentality.

Howard says the core of experienced players are mentoring the youngsters in the US squad and the result is a US team which mixes apparent naivety and boldness – a blend he feels has given them the edge over opponents in the past two years.

MAN IN CHARGE

BOB BRADLEY
Bradley is "Bob the Builder" as far as his squad is concerned. Since the retirement of many of his 2006 generation he has been rebuilding a new fighting force and he is enjoying seeing the youngsters grow in stature in tough international games. Bradley was named as interim coach after the 2006 World Cup finals where he had been Bruce Arena's assistant; then the appointment was made permanent five months later when the US federation's negotiations with Jurgen Klinsmann fell through. At club level Bradley honed his coaching skills at the Chicago Fire and led them to the MLS Cup and US Open Cup double in 1998. It led to Bradley being named MLS Coach of the Year.

ALGERIA

Algeria's return to the World Cup finals after a gap of 24 years may help the north African country erase some bitter memories of a less than edifying experience.

In their first qualification in 1982 the Algerians, one of the strongest African soccer nations of the era, proved a surprise package when they sprang one of the shocks of the Spain tournament with a 2-1 win over European champions West Germany in their opening group game.

But the Germans were to exact their revenge for this ignominious defeat. Although "Les Fennecs" lost 2-0 to Austria and beat Chile 3-2, they were to be eliminated on goal difference after one of the most cynical moves in finals' history when West Germany met Austria.

With the Germans 1-0 up the two German-speaking neighbours realised that if the score stayed the same both would advance at Algeria's expense. The critical sporting media described the rest of a tame match as a "non-aggression pact" but West Germany progressed to the final and Algeria went home early.

The fates were still not with Algeria four years later in Mexico when present coach Rabah Saadane guided them to a consecutive finals' appearance. In a so-called "group of death" they suffered two predictable defeats to Spain and Brazil plus a draw against Northern Ireland and were eliminated.

Even Algeria's 2010 qualifying campaign was not without controversy. Their team bus was attacked on the way from the airport as they drove to meet arch-rivals and close neighbours Egypt in their final group game in Cairo. Algeria's star striker Rafik Saifi was one of four players hurt.

Unbeaten Algeria had already beaten Egypt 3-1 at home and led the group by three points before the Cairo game. Egypt contrived to win 2-0 leaving the two teams joint top with identical records and requiring a play-off.

On neutral territory in the Sudanese city of Omdurman Algeria's centre back Antar Yahia sweetly struck the volley that clinched qualification. Coach Saadane believes he has

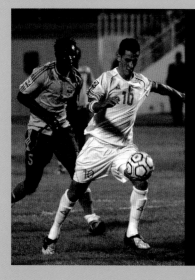

STAR PLAYER

RAFIK SAIFI
Born: February 7, 1975 • **Club:** Al-Khor (Qatar)

At 35 veteran striker Saifi is a much-loved member of the Algerian national squad after more than a decade and over 50 caps. Voted Algeria's Player of the Year in 2008, Saifi remembers some of the struggling sides he has played in and says it is great to see Algeria on the up again and the players smiling. He scored two important qualifying goals and sees the 2010 World Cup finals as the perfect finale to his long career. He has only ever played club soccer in Algeria or France. He won the national title with MC Algiers in 1999 before moving to France later that year where he played more than 100 league games for Troyes and netted 25 goals in 90 league appearances for Lorient.

unearthed and cultivated a core of players who can compete at a high level and make Algeria the African powerhouse it was when it twice qualified in the 1980s.

He said the proof of that is in how well his squad came through their African zone qualifying games and beating not only another of Africa's best, Egypt but also not giving in to provocation.

In the play-off against Egypt, Algeria defended their lead tenaciously and, according to Saadane, "won with dignity."

Saadane singled out two games for special mention as tests of character for his team. In the pre-qualifying group his side fought back from 1-0 down to beat 2002 World Cup quarter-finalists Senegal 3-2; then in an African Cup Group C game a competent 2-0 win in Zambia put Algeria at the top of the group.

Saadane's squad features several players with European experience including midfielder Karim Ziani who plays Champions' League soccer with German high-flyers Wolfsburg while Yahia and forward Karim Mantour are both Bundesliga regulars. Defender Nadir Belhadj has English

Premiership experience with Portsmouth; centre back Bougherra plays for Scottish champions Glasgow Rangers and Rafik Halliche is in Portugal with Nacional. Mansouri and midfield colleague Yacine Bezzaz are in France with Lorient and Strasbourg respectively.

Keeping together the same core of players has paid off for Algeria and their success to date has produced a big wave of enthusiasm and public support for their efforts. Just as in 1982 the squad will not be favourites but they will delight in trying to pull off a surprise or two against the more-fancied sides.

MAN IN CHARGE

RABAH SAADANE

Saadane is now in his fifth term as Algeria's coach. The former defender first took charge in 1981, in time to steer Algeria to the 1982 World Cup finals but, in an amazing turnaround, he was replaced by Rachid Mekloufi before the tournament. But he was back by 1985 and stayed in charge for the 1986 finals. Thirteen years later saw him stepping in again briefly in 1999 then again in 2003. He returned for his present incumbency when he replaced French coach Jean-Michel Cavalli in October 2007 after a slump in performances saw Algeria fail to qualify for the 2008 African Cup of Nations finals.

Group C

SLOVENIA

Tiny Slovenia has been one of the surprise packages of 2010 qualifying. They took on the Russian bear – and won. The reward for this former part of the old Yugoslavia is only their second World Cup appearance.

Beating Russia in a qualifying play-off was a nail-biting affair because Slovenia had been trailing 2-0 with time running out in the Moscow part of the two-legged tie. Then Slovenia substitute Necj Pecnik popped up to head home an 88th minute rebound off Russian goalkeeper Igor Akinfeev to give Slovenia a vital away goal and shift the balance of power back towards the smaller country.

In the second leg in Maribor Zlatko Dedic's 44th-minute winner settled the tie on away goals and it seemed Russia's players had not heeded coach Guus Hiddink who had cautioned them not to underestimate the Slovenes.

Slovenia's slaying of the Russian bear was one of the fairy-tale endings that make for World Cup legends, where a surprise goal can change the situation completely.

Russia did not go out of 2010 World Cup contention without a squabble. They were furious with referee Terje Hauge for sending off Alexander Kerzakhov for a challenge on Slovenia keeper Samir Handanovic and later dismissing Yuri Zhirkov for a second yellow card.

TV replays showed that Slovenia defender Bostjan Cesar and Handanovic were not without blame in the Kerzakhov affair.

Slovenia coach Matjaz Kek described the win as a "triumph for determination and preparation."

Slovenia left it late to come good in the qualifying group but drew upon their strengths when it mattered. The key results were their 3-0 home win over Poland and a surprise 2-0 away victory over eventual group winners Slovakia. Auxerre midfielder Birsa Pecnik, of Portuguese club Nacional provided the goals against Slovakia.

A 3-0 victory in San Marino left Slovenia two points behind the Slovaks and clinched their play-off spot against Russia.

Kek had developed their World Cup bid around a mean defence. Koln's Brecko, Cesar of Grenoble, Ghent's Marko Suler and Sochaux left back Bojan Jokic gelled as a defensive shield in front of Udinese keeper Handanovic to concede just six goals in 12 games. Defensive midfielder Birsa had also come in for praise

STAR PLAYER

ZLATKO DEDIC
Born: October 5, 1984 • **Club:** Bochum (Germany)

Dedic was Slovenia's Russian slayer with the winner against their northern neighbours. The goal, his third all in the qualifiers, qualified Slovenia for South Africa and secured his place in the country's soccer folklore. He also opened the score in their 3-0 win over Poland and was on target in the 1-1 opening draw in Wroclaw. Dedic made his international debut in 2004 but finally established himself as a key player in the qualifying campaign. He joined Parma in 2001 but spent much of his five years there on loan before joining second division Frosinone to earn a regular place. He moved to Bochum in the summer of 2009.

ONES TO WATCH

MILOVOJE NOVAKOVIC

Born: May 18, 1979 • **Club:** Koln (Germany)

The 6ft 4inch striker is all about goals either for club or country. He led Slovenia's scorers in qualifying with five and took his number of international caps to more than 30. He left his home country side Ljubljana in 2002 to play in Austria but made his name after moving to Litex in Bulgaria. He joined Koln in August 2006 and was top scorer with 20 goals when they won promotion to the Bundesliga in 2008.

ROBERT KOREN

Born: September 20, 1980 • **Club:** West Bromwich Albion (England)

A freak incident threatened the Slovenia captain's ability to steer his country successfully through the qualifiers. The attacking midfielder recently suffered a freak training ground injury at his English club West Bromwich Albion which caused loss of vision, but fortunately he made a complete recovery and leads his side to South Africa. He made his international debut in 2003 and has gained more than 40 caps.

for his successful role in screening the back line.

Striker Milivoje Novakovic reckons the forwards played their part in defence, too. He said the Slovenia system was based on everyone closing down the opposition.

There were no huge wins on Slovenia's qualification road and Dedic and Koln's Novakovic were the only players to score more than twice. Pecnik was one of the finds of the qualifiers. He broke into the squad during that time and it is on the cards that Kek will utilise him as an impact sub in South Africa. Robert Koren, Tomsk's Alexander Radosavljevic and Andraz Kirm of Wisla Krakow play more traditional attacking roles.

Slovenia's last World Cup finals' experience – in 2002 – was short-lived even though they were inspired by the man voted their greatest-ever player, Zlatko Zahovic. A trio of defeats to Spain, South Africa and Paraguay saw them fall at the group stage.

Kek says confidence is high among the new generation proudly carrying the Slovenia banner to South Africa, confident they can do better this time. Novakovic has praised the "strong spirit" in the squad. He said there is already a bond among the younger squad players who have come through youth teams together.

In the spirit of the country's relatively new-found independence, Suler is keen to make another point, too. The Slovenia teams which qualified for Euro 2000 and the 2002 World Cup were products of the old Yugoslav system before the various members of the political federation went there various ways.

He says he is proud to be among the first generation to graduate from the burgeoning Slovenian system and hopes they can do it justice in South Africa.

MAN IN CHARGE

MATJAZ KEK

Kek is no stranger to success. He made his name with Maribor, taking over as coach in 2000 after a season as assistant and steered them to league titles in 2001 and 2003. He had already won three Slovenian championships with them as a player. His success in getting the national side to South Africa has been put down to his meticulous planning and attention to detail. Kek cut his international coaching teeth in charge of the Slovenia under-15 and under-16 teams in 2006 before he succeeded Branko Oblak as national coach early in 2007. Although Slovenia failed to qualify for Euro 2008 from a group dominated by Romania and Holland, Kek has repaid the faith in him by turning a new young team into surprise World Cup qualifiers.

GERMANY

A check on the history of German participation in the World Cup finals reveals that the two always go together. South Africa is no different and Germany are among the favourites – as usual.

Germany, either pre World War 2 or later as West Germany, have competed in 16 of the 18 finals. With typical Teutonic efficiency they have consistently made the final stages their own. Champions three times, runners up four times, three third places, a fourth place and three quarter finals is one of the most enviable records in soccer history

In short no World Cup finals would be complete without formidable Germany.

These masters of tournament soccer did it again for 2010 coming through their European qualifying group with typical thoroughness. They polished off minnows Liechtenstein, Azerbaijan and Wales and still had enough left over to win both games against their main rivals Russia.

Full back Philipp Lahm believes it is Germany's illustrious history that spurs every new squad to a special mental strength with each successive generation eager to wear the famous black and white strip.

With World Cup wins in 1954, 1974 and 1990 and European Championship success in 1972, 1980 and 1996, players and supporters have grown up with the conviction that a German team is always good enough to reach the final.

Miroslav Klose's 48th international goal clinched the 1-0 victory in Moscow which saw Germany to South Africa for another crack at the World Cup with a game to spare. Surviving the last 21 minutes with 10 men after defender Jerome Boateng was sent off meant Germany showed nerves of steel that day and their famous resilience paid off. Russia ultimately failed to qualify after a play-off.

Germany's recent record in international tournaments – third in the 2006 World Cup and runners-up at Euro 2008 – seems to indicate that they are ready again for the ultimate prize in 2010.

Germany combines technical quality and physical strength to combat the six or seven teams around the world which play better soccer.

STAR PLAYER

MICHAEL BALLACK
Born: September 26, 1976 • **Club:** Chelsea (England)

He hopes that South Africa 2010 will end the jinx that has cursed him in major finals. He was captain of the teams which lost to Italy in the 2006 World Cup semi finals and to Spain at Euro 2008. He was also on the losing side in UEFA Champions League finals with Bayer Leverkusen in 2002 and his current club Chelsea in 2008. Ballack is approaching 100 caps and as, captain since 2004, he is hoping to be the man to lift the World Cup trophy for Germany in 2010. From his midfield role he scored Germany's 2002 World Cup semi-final winner against South Korea but a yellow card from that match kept him out of the 2-0 defeat by Brazil in the Final. There has been speculation about his impending international retirement after South Africa.

ONES TO WATCH

MIROSLAV KLOSE

Born: June 9, 1978 • **Club:** Bayern Munich (Germany)

Poland's loss was Germany's gain when the Polish-born striker decided in 2001 to play for his father's homeland. Klose has become one of Germany's most prolific scorers and is a man who comes good for World Cup matches. He scored five as Germany reached the 2002 World Cup final and repeated the feat again as top scorer at the 2006 finals tournament.

BASTIAN SCHWEINSTEIGER

Born: August 1, 1984 • **Club:** Bayern Munich (Germany)

One of the players who has adjusted his game to coach Joachim Low's new game plan. Originally a combative defensive midfielder, Schweinsteiger has recently played a more attacking role. His versatility in midfield has gained him more than 70 caps including Germany's run to a World Cup third place in 2006 and in the Euro 2008 final. Schweinsteiger was a talented skier as well as a promising soccer player.

They have a few individuals who can turn a match when things look bad.

Lahm is a brilliant attacking full back and captain and midfield star Michael Ballack has scored over 40 goals for Germany, including four in the qualifiers. Bastian Schweinsteiger has begun to contribute important goals but tipped as his country's rising star is Mesut Ozil. Observers say the 21-year-old is developing all the qualities to be a world-class No 10. Elsewhere in midfield, Germany has experienced Piotr Trochowski and Thomas Hitzlsperger with young hopeful Thomas Muller winning more and more caps for his country.

Up front, Klose is a prolific scorer of important goals and netted seven goals in the qualifiers. His partnership with Lukas Podolski who hit the target six times in qualifying is one of Germany's great strengths.

The strikers were recently stung by criticism from Gerd Muller, the great striker whose goal won the 1974 final, but coach Joachim Low rushed to their defence saying that despite the art of defending becoming more sophisticated across the world game these two were still scoring regularly.

That Germany conceded only five goals in 10 qualifying ties is testament to their own defensive methods. Goalkeeper Rene Adler has established himself as the successor to Oliver Kahn and Jens Lehmann. Midfielder Simon Rolfes shields the back line, which is built around experienced centre back Per Mertesacker and veteran full back Arne Friedrich.

With victorious past teams under masters such Franz Beckenbauer very much in mind, Low says he is sure that a German squad will reach those levels again. He will no doubt be hoping it will be during his tenure and in South Africa in 2010.

MAN IN CHARGE

JOACHIM LOW

Low, Jurgen Klinsmann's assistant at the 2006 finals, has rebuilt the German team over the past 18 months. He proved his vision of a team which used a blend of technique and physical power worked when it took Germany to the Euro 2008 final. Low is likely to repeat the formula in South Africa despite criticism in some quarters of the media. He has introduced young players such as Mesut Ozil, Jerome Boateng, Thomas Muller and full back Andreas Beck. Building this team has not been easy for Low who needed diplomatic skills to resolve a punch up between Podolski and Ballack. He also showed his toughness in ending Kevin Kuranyi's international career after a halftime walk-out by the striker.

Group D

AUSTRALIA

Australia qualified for South Africa via an Asian group for the first time. Elevation to 21st in the world rankings has renewed their faith that they can improve on their last World Cup finals' appearance.

Australia's "Socceroos" arrived in the South Africa finals by a different and more direct route this time. They "escaped" to the Asian Confederation after the 2006 World Cup and qualified direct for the first time. Previously the Australians had come through the qualifiers in FIFA's far-flung Oceana region but had not been happy to find themselves often in a play-off against a South American side.

This time the plan worked as they qualified from Asian Group One with two games to spare. The Australians pre-qualified from a group including Qatar, China and Asian champions Iraq, then topped their final group unbeaten, with six wins and two draws.

Australia's smooth passage to South Africa contrasts vividly with their qualification four years earlier when goalkeeper Mark Schwarzer was the hero of the penalty shoot-out win over Uruguay which took Australia to Germany. The new route to the finals did not take away the sense of achievement according to Schwarzer. He said qualifying this time was still an emotional moment.

Galatasaray midfielder Harry Kewell, who has English Premiership experience with Leeds and Liverpool reckons the new format worked to Australian advantage with the games just as intense.

Australia topped their qualifying group thanks to a string of fine closing results, including a 0-0 draw away to Qatar in Doha, a 2-0 home win over Bahrain, and a 2-1 victory over Japan in which Cahill scored twice as the Socceroos came from behind in front of 70,000 fans in Melbourne.

There is a strong belief in the squad that they can better their second-round finish in Germany in 2006 and very few teams will look forward to playing this well organised and committed team.

Initially there had been criticism of Dutch coach Pim Verbeek's seemingly-cautious tactics

68

STAR PLAYER

TIM CAHILL
Born: December 6, 1979 • **Club:** Everton (England)

Cahill's nickname is "The Invisible Man" for his habit of using his powerful spring to score spectacular headers while eluding defenders. At 5'10" (1.78m) he is smaller than most of his markers but powers in almost unseen with well-timed late runs to score. The Everton midfielder has been described as one of the best players to come out from Down Under and was the first Australian to score in World Cup finals when he shot an 84th-minute equaliser against Japan at Germany 2006. He added a second five minutes later, then set up John Aloisi for a 3-1 win. He also hit a double against Japan to ensure Australia finished top of their 2010 qualifying group.

ONES TO WATCH

MARK SCHWARZER
Born: October 6, 1972 • **Club:** Fulham (England)

Schwarzer's superstition of always wearing the same shin pads he had on at his professional debut seems to be paying off. At 38 he is playing as well as ever in the English Premier League and for his country. He commands his penalty area, has a fine understanding with his defenders and can make match-turning saves. He became a national hero with two penalty saves against Uruguay which sent Australia to the 2006 finals.

BRETT EMERTON
Born: February 22, 1979 • **Club:** Blackburn Rovers (England)

Emerton's return to the Australia squad in 2009 after a serious cruciate ligament injury that needed surgery was greeted with delight –especially by coach Pim Verbeek. The Blackburn Rovers star is a real asset to his country. He is fast, direct and can double up at right midfield or wing back. He has also scored valuable goals, including two against Qatar in Australia's 4-0 home qualifying win.

of selecting two holding midfielders. But he maintains that his sides always attacked with a minimum of five players.

But there was also a depth of strength in defence and testament to that is that they conceded just one goal in those eight games. The back line has been well marshalled by captain Lucas Neill with Blackburn Rover's Vince Grella and ex-PSV Eindhoven star Jason Culina standing firm with him.

Neill cites focus as the attribute making Australia hard to beat throughout the campaign. At the other end, the lack of a prolific scorer has been a concern since 2006 captain Mark Viduka quit the international scene through injury. In qualifying for South Africa Palermo midfielder Mark Bresciano's 93rd-minute winner in Bahrain was one of only 12 goals the Aussies scored.

The finals in South Africa may be the chance for the giant Josh Kennedy of Japanese league club Grampus Eight to step up to the plate as Australia's spearhead. He had already scored in home wins over Qatar and Uzbekistan.

Verbeek will expect Cahill, Kewell and Blackburn's Brett Emerton to add goals from midfield, something that they have proved they can do well for their clubs. A quarter-final place will, no doubt, please the Australians and their supporters.

They will not be the surprise package this time in South Africa but the core of the 2006 team will be there packing a great deal more experience thanks to their employment in European leagues.

MAN IN CHARGE

PIM VERBEEK
Verbeek has stepped into the limelight as a coach in his own right after two previous World Cups as assistant. He was Guus Hiddink's assistant in sensationally taking South Korea to the last four in 2002 and number 2 to Dick Advocaat when South Korea qualified for Germany 2006. He says steering Australia to South Africa 2010 is his greatest achievement but does not care about his off-pitch popularity nor justifying a no-nonsense approach to his work. He had hoped to blood local Australian A-League players for the current Asian Cup qualifying campaign to protect his overseas stars. But, after having to call up his regulars because of poor early results, he sparked a fierce debate when he questioned the A-League's quality. He said that he felt Australia's more-promising players should go to Europe to develop because the league standards are higher there.

SERBIA

The changing geography of eastern Europe over the past 20 years means that Serbia arrive at a World Cup finals in their third incarnation. Their task in South Africa 2010 is to re-establish their country as a strong regional soccer power.

As Yugoslavia, the country made eight World Cup appearances and twice reached the semi-finals; as Serbia and Montenegro in 2006 their World Cup was a disaster.

Now new coach Radomir "Raddy" Antic and his squad have the chance to re-establish Serbia ahead of bitter rivals and neighbours Croatia who had failed to get to South Africa. They will also want to erase the memory of their appearance in Germany in 2006 where they were eliminated at the group stage. Defeats by Holland and Ivory Coast and a 6-0 hammering by Argentina dented national pride.

It is just plain Serbia now as Serbia and Montenegro split in June 2006 and the South Africa campaign will be a first as an independent state.

That pride was damaged before at France 1998 when, as Yugoslavia, they lost 2-1 to Holland in the last 16 while the Croats reached the semi-finals.

Antic says he is setting no targets for his squad in South Africa but that he had achieved an objective by qualifying. He admits Serbian morale was sinking when he ended a four-year retirement from a long and successful club management career to take over the national squad in 2008.

He inherited a squad that had failed to qualify for Euro 2008, yet seen Croatia reach the quarter finals. To compound the national soccer depression the under-23 squad had flopped at the Beijing Olympics.

Changes were made and it was a more confident Serbia under Antic which eased past favourites France to top European qualifying Group Seven. Croatia were eliminated in another group headed by England and Ukraine.

Superior away form was crucial to Serbia for 2010. Despite losing in Paris and drawing 1-1 with the French in Belgrade, Serbia put together wins in Austria and Romania. Meanwhile Austria defeated the French in Vienna and Romania held them to two draws.

Routing the Romanians 5-0 meant Serbia qualified

STAR PLAYER

DEJAN STANKOVIC
Born: September 11, 1978 • **Club:** Internazionale (Italy)

Stankovic leads as Serbia's captain by example. He is a tough tackler, a clever strategist capable of splitting defences with a single pass and is also Serbia's free kick expert, with a powerful shot. The defensive central midfielder has forged a career with 12 seasons so far at the top of Italy's Serie A and has notched up more than 80 appearances with his national team. He believes Serbia have yet to fulfil their international potential and after an impressive run to the South Africa finals the squad does not want to let the fans down.

ONES TO WATCH

NEMANJA VIDIC
Born: October 21, 1981 • **Club:** Manchester United (England)

When the going gets tough, Vidic is the man to call. He is a tough, mobile stopper who is strong in the air and poses a serious threat at free-kick situations. Centre back Vidic is a key figure for club and country with a taste for success after winning the European Champions' League and three Premiership titles with United.

MILAN JOVANOVIC
Born: April 18, 1981 • **Club:** Standard Liege (Belgium)

Prolific scoring is Jovanovic's forte. He led Serbia's scorers with five goals in qualifying and has been knocking them in for Standard Liege since 2006. Voted Belgium's Player of the Year in 2008, he likes to operate as a second striker, arriving late in the box. He was almost unknown to many Serb fans when coach Javier Clemente gave him his international debut in 2007.

forward. Winger Krasic offers trickery on the right while giant 2.03m (6ft 8in) forward Nikola Zigic spearheads the attack with Milan Jovanovic.

There is a great deal of weight on some of these young shoulders; they not only have to resurrect their country's soccer fortunes but also transform its image after the various Balkan conflicts it was involved in during the 1990s.

with a game to spare and skipper Dejan Stankovic felt the team had hit new heights. They lost only two qualifiers, including a meaningless last game in Lithuania.

The Serbian job was the first international post for Antic who was a respected club coach in Spain for 16 years with Real Madrid, Barcelona and Atletico Madrid. He admitted becoming national coach of his homeland was a challenge he relished and set about creating close to a club spirit within the national squad.

He believes they will fly to South Africa with a big family atmosphere and confidence high.

Centre back Nemanja Vidic, adored by Manchester United fans the world over, is one of a new crop of players that have helped transform Serbia's fortunes and he believes the backbone of the current squad will still be playing together by the time the Brazil 2014 World Cup comes around.

Antic said it was key that he was able to name virtually the same squad for several qualifiers. A change of club for goalkeeper Vladimir Stojkovic is getting him regular soccer and Branislav Ivanovic of Chelsea has built a fine understanding with Vidic. Young Borussia Dortmund defender Neven Subotic provides cover for them. Internazionale's Stankovic runs the midfield and provides opportunities for Nenad Milijas' breaks

MAN IN CHARGE

RADOMIR "RADDY" ANTIC
Transforming Serbia's fortunes was Antic's first national team job after years in the club game, especially in Spain. Serbia's impressive qualification has been a triumph for Antic, the one-time midfielder who took over after Miroslav Dukic was sacked following Serbia's poor performance at the 2008 Olympics. Antic was able to coach Serbia while commuting from his long-time home in Spain where he is something of a legend.

After retiring as a defender with Zaragosa he became the only man who has coached not only Real Madrid but also their two greatest rivals, Barcelona and Atletico Madrid.

GHANA

The bookmakers have been taking bets on an African team making a huge impact on the first World Cup finals held in Africa. Ghana, nicknamed the Black Stars, is determined to live up to that billing.

Ghana caused a sensation the only time they have been to a World Cup finals stage – in 2006 – and the memory is still sweet for their ever-improving squad who want to go several steps better this time.

Such was the Ghanaians keenness to play in South Africa they threw themselves determinedly into the task and became the first African nation to qualify, with a 2-0 home win over Sudan in Accra.

They had already created a sensation in their first finals' appearance in 2006. Stung by losing to eventual champions Italy in their opening group game, they shocked the Czech Republic 2-0, then beat the United States 2-1 to reach the last 16 – where there was no disgrace in being eliminated by Brazil.

Under new coach Milovan Rajevac, who was appointed to what was his first overseas soccer job in 2008, Ghana, the African champions of 1963, 1965, 1978 and 1982, want to prove they are more than just a former regional power. Booking a ticket for the relatively-short hop across Africa from Ghana to South Africa became a crusade for the squad according to Serbian-born Rajevac. For his hungry squad, he says, 2006's performances were just for starters.

Ghana packs some exceptional talent such as midfield star Michael Essien. International playing experience is a strong thread throughout the squad. Defenders John Mensah and John Pantsil, plus the formidable midfield trio of Essien, Sulley Muntari and skipper Stephen Appiah and strikers Matthew Amoah, Eric Addo and Gyan Asamoah have all played in the top echelons of English, German and French soccer.

Mensah is one of those backing a sensation from an African team in South Africa – obviously hoping that things will go the way of Ghana and he will be part of it.

STAR PLAYER

MICHAEL ESSIEN
Born: December 3, 1982 • **Club:** Chelsea (England)

As the costliest African player, the £24.5million Chelsea paid for Michael Essien bought them vibrant energy, dynamism, versatility and the ability to score from outside the box. These are the qualities he also brings to the Ghana team and have made him the poster boy of Ghanaian soccer. Local fans take huge pride in his achievements, regarding him as "a gift from God", and his presence lifts the players around him. If Essien can control his impulse for the rash challenges which get him yellow cards, Ghana could gets it wish to be the most-influential African nation at the 2010 finals.

ONES TO WATCH

SULLEY MUNTARI

Born: Konongo, August 27, 1984 • **Club:** Internazionale (Italy)

If there are any concerns about Muntari it is his disciplinary record. He was sent off three times while playing for Udinese in 2006-7 but as he is one of Ghana's most important players they want him to stay on the pitch in South Africa. He combines strength with craft, runs tirelessly from box to box and has an eye for a goal as he showed with the opener in Ghana's decisive 2-0 win over Sudan.

MATTHEW AMOAH

Born: October 24, 1980 • **Club:** NAC Breda (Holland)

Three of Matthew Amoah's goals in consecutive matches propelled Ghana through to the 2006 finals and he did it again when his double strike against Sudan in Omdurman virtually clinched Ghana's South Africa finals' slot. Amoah is a favourite with his club Breda and has proved his consistency at the top of the Dutch league by netting more than 100 goals.

With Essien at its heart, midfield is Ghana's strength and World Cup watchers will probably see a different Essien playing with more freedom for his country than he does for Chelsea.

The ever-reliable midfield anchoring by Anthony Annan frees Essien to exploit his natural power, strength and elegance and Annan is full of praise for his colleague – describing him as "an amazing player." Essien also gets vital goals for Ghana as he does at club level.

Inter's Muntari is a combative presence and Appiah has battled a series of knee injuries while continuing to shine for his beloved national team.

Ghana's qualification was not a breeze, their 2-0 win over Sudan was the culmination of a determined campaign which in the preliminary African group matches saw them struggle and lose to Libya and Gabon. Only a 3-2 win in Lesotho saw them through.

It was significant that Essien was injured for that part of the competition. When he returned for the final group stage Ghana chalked up more-superior performances and away wins in Mali and Sudan put them in command.

Rajevac had prepared for the trip to Sudan by taking the team to a special training camp in Kenya which had the hot and humid conditions the Ghanaians would face in Omdurman.

Rajevac and his team also learned a lesson about complacency after a surprise result just three days following their qualification for South Africa.

They led Japan 3-1 in a friendly in the Dutch city of Utrecht with two goals from Asamoah, the other by Amoah, then they conceded three in 13 minutes to lose 4-3. Rajevac admits a series of substitutions weakened his team's cohesion, something that he will remember at the World Cup finals.

MAN IN CHARGE

MILOVAN RAJEVAC

After spending all his career in the former Yugoslavia or the new Serbia, Rajevac took his first overseas coaching job in Ghana in August 2008. It was a brave move because he was initially in for a rough ride with criticism over early defeats and his failure to speak English.

After World Cup qualifying defeats in Gabon and Libya he won over the players, kept a settled side and achieved results where it mattered in the second qualifying phase. He waived a signing-on fee when he took over as Ghana coach but was confident enough about his abilities to ensure he had a World Cup qualifying bonus in his contract said to be worth around $500,000.

NETHERLANDS

One of the big questions at every World Cup finals is: "Will the Netherlands fulfill their potential this time." Once again a Holland side is bursting with talent but will it succeed where even the great Johann Cruyff failed?

The Dutch, often riven by internal differences, are the nearly men of world cup soccer who have failed to deliver despite teams studded with world-class talent and among the best coaches.

Twice in the Netherland's soccer playing history they have lost World Cup finals – to West Germany in 1974 and Argentina in 1978 – in an era of what was dubbed the greatest Holland team of all, led by their greatest player of all, Johan Cruyff.

The Holland World Cup hoodoo struck again in 1998, when they lost their semi-final to Brazil in a penalty shoot-out.

Outside the World Cup they have also flattered to deceive when they lost a European Championship semi-final on penalties to Denmark in 1992 and to 10-man Italy, in their home city of Rotterdam, at the same stage of Euro 2000.

The Dutch dressing room discord is legendary and 1970's midfield general Wim van Hanegem once said: "We think there's a problem if we don't have a problem!"

However, at Euro 88 coach Rinus Michels showed that imposing rigid discipline on a team of huge talent and egos can work. His team featuring Ruud Gullit, Frank Rijkaard, Ronald Koeman and Marco Van Basten fulfilled their huge potential when goals from Gullit and van Basten gave the Netherlands a 2-0 final victory over the USSR.

At South Africa 2010 repeating that task faces coach Bert Van Marwijk. Holland's 2-1 win in Iceland in June 2009 saw them as the first European side to qualify, having won all eight group games – against Iceland, Norway, Macedonia and Scotland – with an impressive goal difference of 17-2.

Van Marwijk says he has instilled organisation and a ruthless streak which has made the defensive record so superb. Some eyebrows were raised when he recalled his son-in-law, Mark

STAR PLAYER

ROBIN VAN PERSIE
Born: Rotterdam, Holland, August 6, 1983 • **Club:** Arsenal (England)

A recurrence of his persistent knee problems could rob Holland of the undoubted talents of Van Persie. His left foot is one of the most potent weapons in international soccer and he has immense skill on the ball and a powerful shot. He is versatile and can play as a lead striker – as he has recently for both his club Arsenal and Holland – or he can operate behind a front man or attack from the wings. Van Persie has a history of clashes with Van Marwijk but they have called a truce, it seems, in the interests of national need. The player left Feyenoord for Arsenal after Van Marwijk demoted him to the reserves.

WESLEY SNEIJDER

Born: June 9, 1984 • **Club:** Internazionale (Italy)

The two-footed Sneijder has a point to prove after being displaced from his Real Madrid career by Kaka's summer 2009 arrival. The World Cup finals could be just the stage for Holland's midfield creative force to make his case. He is quick, strong, sees opportunities early and can deliver pinpoint passes over any distance. Defences also need to be very watchful when Sneijder shapes up to take free kicks.

ARJEN ROBBEN

Born: January 23, 1984 • **Club:** Bayern Munich (Germany)

Robben was another talented Dutchman to suffer from Real Madrid's 2009 creation of their new Galacticos squad. The Spaniards sold him to Bayern Munich to make way for Cristiano Ronaldo. A left-footed winger, Robben has a mesmerising dribbling technique and a good scoring record for club and country. If he has a fault in his game it is over-elaboration.

looking for their national side to go all the way in South Africa. It will be a true resurrection for a country which gave birth to the "Total Football" concept of the 1970s yet actually failed even to qualify for the 2002 finals in the Far East after losing 1-0 to a 10-man Republic of Ireland side in Dublin.

Van Bommel, to the midfield anchor role but the qualifying results speak for themselves on that decision. Van Bommel can be joined by Nigel De Jong if a containment strategy is required.

Rafael Van der Vaart and Wesley Sneijder are Holland's midfield creators for Dirk Kuyt and Arjen Robben on the wings and strikers such as Robin Van Persie or Klaas-Jan Huntelaar.

A boost for the Dutch has been Real Madrid's Ruud Van Nistelrooy's decision to come out of international retirement as he bids to add in South Africa to his 33 Holland goals.

That cornucopia of Dutch talent has given Van Marwijk confidence in going all the way in 2010 but he knows the finals will not be the easy ride they had in qualifying.

Skipper and left back Giovanni van Bronckhorst has told his team they will have to be on top form throughout. Much depends on the Van Marwijk squad maintaining their newly-acquired mental toughness and the winning habit.

Van Marwijk's assistant and former international Frank De Boer tasted some of Holland's near-miss experiences and now says it is the mission of the current squad to be world champions. He believes they can be if they can maintain the form and attitude of their European group qualifiers.

The soccer-mad Dutch public will certainly be

MAN IN CHARGE

BERT VAN MARWIJK

Bert Van Marwijk, who steered Feyenoord to the UEFA Cup in 2002, has subtly changed the Dutch approach from the days of Marco van Basten. He has emphasised defensive discipline and the importance of maintaining a compact unit alongside Holland's traditional flair. Public expectations of finally winning the World Cup are high throughout Holland following their 100 per cent qualification record. The Dutch football federation's (KNVB) hopes for a place at least in the last four, have not frightened Van Marwijk from making controversial decisions or using the time Holland's early qualification has given him to experiment.

DENMARK

Denmark's Morten Olsen will be a man with a special mission in South Africa. The captain of the Danish side which failed in the 1986 finals returns as coach of his national side and hoping for a different outcome.

Olsen is determined to redress the collapse in the last 16 of 1986 and Denmark's failing to qualify for the Germany 2006 and Euro 2008 finals. He says there is a new confidence in his side after beating favourites Portugal to the top spot of their European qualifying group without star centre back Martin Laursen who retired because of persistent knee injuries.

Denmark nicknamed themselves "Landshold X" ("National team X") because they lacked star names. Yet they qualified with a game to spare after an incredible victory in Portugal plus two wins over old rivals and Scandinavian neighbours Sweden which had given the unfancied Danes a flying start.

Denmark's 3-2 win surprised Portugal's star line-up in Lisbon and demonstrated their Viking resilience. It was all done in a late surge with Arsenal striker Nicklas Bendtner equalising Nani's opening goal with seven minutes left. Deco restored Portugal's lead from the penalty spot but Christian Poulsen reflected the Danish never-say-die attitude by levelling in the 88th minute and Daniel Jensen grabbed the winner in the second minute of added stoppage time.

This victory gave Denmark an early advantage over the favourites, which they reinforced with a 1-1 home draw.

Denmark did the "double" over Sweden with Thomas Kahlenberg's goal clinching victory in Sweden and Jakob Poulsen's strike seeing off the Swedes in Copenhagen.

Olsen has devoted almost 29 years of his life to his national team as a player or coach and he feels the current squad has a point to prove. After failing to qualify for the 2006 World Cup finals and Euro 2008, Danish supporters have been starved of major tournaments and the team reckoned they owed it to their fans to qualify for South Africa.

The memory Olsen really wants to improve on is 1986 as a player with Denmark in their first-ever World Cup finals appearance. Denmark had a "special generation" of players including Jesper

STAR PLAYER

CHRISTIAN POULSEN
Born: February 28, 1980 • **Club:** Juventus (Italy)

Though self-discipline can be a problem with the combative Poulsen he remains a key man for Denmark. Although brilliant in his role as midfield organiser, defensive protector and tenacious man marker, discipline has been a blind spot. At the 2002 World Cup finals two yellow cards earned him a ban and, in a Euro 2008 qualifier, he was also red-carded for punching an opponent and suspended for three matches. But his wholehearted contribution to Denmark is vital as he also occasionally darts forward to score, as he showed in the 3-2 away win over Portugal. He has proved himself at the highest levels of European soccer with Juventus and was the first man to be voted Denmark's Player of the Year in successive seasons in 2005 and 2006.

ONES TO WATCH

THOMAS SORENSEN
Born: June 12, 1976 • **Club:** Stoke City (England)

Sorensen had the massive task of succeeding Denmark's most-capped player, and former world No 1 goalkeeper, Peter Schmeichel and has done it impressively. He has proved his credentials as a brilliant shot stopper in the Schmeichel mould by winning more than 80 Danish caps and being an English Premiership regular over 10 years.

NICKLAS BENDTNER
Born: January 16, 1988 • **Club:** Arsenal (England)

Bendtner is one of Denmark's "young guns" and established himself as Denmark's leading striker during the qualifiers. At 6ft 4in tall and strong in the air, he spearheads the Danish attack. His club Arsenal has recognised his surprising mobility for his size and use him as a raider from the right. More club opportunities since Emmanuel Adebayor's departure means Bendtner has grown in confidence from which Olsen said Denmark have benefited.

Olsen, Michael Laudrup, Preben Elkjaer, Soren Lerby and Frank Arnesen and sailed through their group.

They beat Scotland 1-0, Uruguay 6-1 and the mighty West Germany 2-0 but midfield general Arnesen was sent off against the Germans and missed the last-16 game against Spain. Denmark were annihilated by Emiliano Butragueno's four goals as Spain won 5-1.

Denmark had blazed brightly for a short while in 1986 then were extinguished and the like was not to be seen again until the 1992 European Championship final when the Danes again shocked favourites Germany to win 2-0.

Veteran forward Jon Dahl Tomasson said 1986 and 1992 proved Denmark could compete against the world and play great soccer. Other international bright spots for Denmark were the 2002 World Cup finals when Olsen's team topped their group and beat 1998 champions France, only to lose 3-0 to England in the last 16. Four years earlier they had reached the quarter finals and showed great strength despite narrowly losing 3-2 to Brazil.

While on paper not looking as illustrious as the "special generation" the current Denmark squad is highly rated by Olsen and he has several promising young stars such as Bendtner and Simon Kjaer.

Palermo's Kjaer and Daniel Agger of Liverpool have formed a formidable centre-back partnership, in front of long-serving goalkeeper Thomas Sorensen.

For experience Denmark can rely on Fiorentina midfielder Martin Jorgensen who is a veteran of 1998 and 2002 and Feyenoord's Tomasson netted four of Denmark's five goals in the 2002 World Cup finals.

Tough-tackling Christian Poulsen of Juventus will shield the back four in South Africa where the Danes will look to Bendtner and Duisburg's Soren Larsen for a good supply of goals. Larsen led their 2010 qualifying scorers with five and Bendtner three.

MAN IN CHARGE

MORTEN OLSEN

Olsen is one of the world's longest-serving international coaches, having been appointed by Denmark in 2000. Only Olsen's 1986 World Cup coach Sepp Piontek has served longer in the modern era. Olsen got the job after a very successful club career as a defender – he was the first Danish player to reach 100 caps – and coach. He was Denmark's Player of the Year in 1983 and 1986, though he played virtually the whole of his career in Belgium and West Germany. After leaving FC Koln, he coached Brondby to two Danish titles and the 1991 UEFA Cup semis. He was then out of soccer for two years before Ajax hired him in 1997 to steer them to a Dutch league and cup double.

JAPAN

The pressure is on Japan because coach Takeshi Okada has publicly targeted a semi-final spot for a country that has never got past the second round in 12 years of trying.

Okada's optimism is shared by his team. After clinching qualification in Uzbekistan, the players sprayed Okada with champagne and chanted that they will "surprise the world."

Japan have been Asian champions in 2000 and 2004 but they found the step up to the World Cup finals a much-harder task even as hosts in 2002 when they fell in the second round. The beaten Japanese squad had to sit and watch co-hosts South Korea become the only Asian team ever to reach the semi-finals.

Japan followed up Okada's ambitious declaration by crashing 3-0 to the Netherlands while on a European tour, then recovered from a 3-1 deficit to beat Ghana 4-3 a few days later. Although critics have rubbished the coach's dream as unrealistic, Okada believes meeting 2010 contenders such as Holland and Ghana is the sort of experience vital to his side's ability to improve before the finals.

Backed by loyal midfield star Shunsuke Nakamura, he is convinced it will raise Japan's level but history is against them in their task.

They have never won a finals match outside their own country and Okada was in charge when they lost to Argentina, Croatia and Jamaica in the group stage at France 1998.

Eight years later, when coached by Brazilian star Zico, Japan lost 3-1 to Australia, drew 0-0 with Croatia, then crashed 4-1 to Brazil in the group games in Germany.

Japan scored their only wins – 1-0 against Russia and 2-0 over Tunisia –when they were co-hosts in 2002. They went out 1-0 to Turkey in the last 16.

Qualifying for South Africa was achieved with relative ease behind Australia who had switched from the Oceana group. Japan's 1-0 win in Uzbekistan carried them through with two games to spare.

Midfield is seen as Japan's strongest area but one of its problem areas has been coming by goals; they scored only 11 in their eight qualifying matches.

Shinjo Okazaki hit the winner to narrowly defeat Uzbekistan in Tashkent but that was his only strike. Of

STAR PLAYER

SHUNSUKE NAKAMURA
Born: June 24, 1978 • **Club:** Espanyol (Spain)

Nakamura is the most successful Japanese soccer export since Hidetoshi Nakata, the midfield general he succeeded in the national team. Nakamura is the creative hub of Japan's industrious midfield and has an accurate left foot and an eye for a scoring opportunity. His dipping free kicks have fooled many a defensive wall. Nakamura was voted Player of the Tournament both times Japan won the Asian Cup in 2000 and 2004. The tactics of 2002 coach Philippe Troussier left no room for Nakamura's particular style so he missed out on the World Cup finals on home soil. New coach Zico quickly restored him to the national side and Nakamura now has more than 90 caps to cherish.

79

ONES TO WATCH

JUNICHI INAMOTO
Born: September 18, 1979 • **Club:** Rennes (France)

This tough-tackling midfielder was a rising star of the Japan side which won the Asian Cup in 2000 but is now one of the most experienced members of the current squad with more than 70 caps to his name. Expected to play a holding role in South Africa, he has been to two successful World Cup finals' tournaments with Japan, in 2002 when he scored twice, and in 2006.

YUJI NAKAZAWA
Born: February 25, 1978 • **Club:** Yokohama F Marinos (Japan)

Centre back and skipper Nakazawa is back after retiring from international soccer following the 2006 World Cup finals. Former coach Ivan Osim persuaded him to rejoin the squad in 2007 and he is now a vital part of latest coach Takeshi Okada's strategy for South Africa. He trained with Brazilian club America Mineiro for a year before returning to Japan and played in Japan's Asian Cup-winning sides of 2000 and 2004 but was left out of the 2002 World Cup squad

other players considered likely to contribute goals Keiji Tamada netted just twice and Yoshito Okubo did not make the net bulge at all.

In the wings is the Catania striker Takayuki Morimoto who offers Okada another option, but his chances and availability have been limited by injuries and club commitments. Japan's coach will continue his experiment through a series of globetrotting friendlies but he must also think of qualifying for the 2011 Asian Cup finals. Okada's plans to use only Japanese domestic J League players for the Asian Cup qualifying competition were derailed by a 1-0 defeat in Bahrain which forced him to rethink and to call up his Europe-based stars.

Across Europe he has a string of experienced players who have forged their names in some very competitive leagues. They include Wolfsburg's Makoto Hasebe, Venlo's Keisuke Honda and Saint-Etienne winger Daisuke Matsui who offer experience in midfield to complement Nakamura and his partner, Yasuhito Endo, from Gamba Osaka.

Okada has been considering FC Tokyo's Naohiro Ishikawa as cover for injury-prone Matsui and tough-tackling Junichi Inamoto remains ever-reliable in front of the back four where captain and reliable stopper Yuji Nakazawa and Marcus Tanaka anchor the defence.

Tanaka was born in Sao Paulo to a Brazilian-Japanese father and moved to Japan when he was 15. He offers Okada other options by being able to operate as a conventional centre back, a sweeper behind Nakazawa or as a defensive midfielder.

His versatility doesn't end there; he also has a knack of chipping in with goals from free kicks, including two in the qualifiers – something which might prove valuable if the Japanese strikers continue to be goal shy.

MAN IN CHARGE

TAKESHI OKADA

Okada put pressure on himself and his squad when he confidently stated that Japan's 2010 target was the semi-finals. He has returned 12 years after he steered Japan to their first finals' appearance at France 1998 where they were eliminated at the group stage after losing all three matches and Okada was replaced by Philippe Troussier.

Okada returned to take over the national team in December 2007 after Ivan Osim's stroke and has guided them comfortably to their fourth consecutive finals where he has stated his high hopes for them.

Between spells with the national team the former Japan defender coached Yokohama F Marinos to successive J League championships in 2003 and 2004 and was named Manager of the Year both years.

CAMEROON

African World Cup pioneers Cameroon will be looking to at least equal their headline-hitting exploits of Italia 1990 when they and star player Roger Milla became the first African side to reach the World Cup quarter-finals.

There are many who believe that the African soccer revolution will come to fruition in the 2010 finals. Several of South Africa's fellow African nations, as well as the host country itself, have the best chance yet to show that the continent's best is as good as the rest of the world – and Cameroon will be one of those out to prove it.

Former Cameroon coach Otto Pfister, who took them to the 2008 African Nations Cup final, believes African soccer has come on in leaps and bounds and an African team has a realistic chance of reaching the semi finals in 2010.

Pfister was succeeded by Paul Le Guen who needed all his inspirational skills to lift Cameroon spirits after a shock defeat by Togo and a home draw with Morocco early in the qualifying campaign.

Le Guen, who had a pedigree for bringing through African talent in his club coaching job at Rennes in France, says pressure comes as standard with the Cameroon coaching role and that resurrecting the qualifying chances of the "Indomitable Lions" was part of the territory.

He went on to lead Cameroon to qualification with four straight wins, starting with a 2-0 victory away to their toughest group rivals, Gabon. Achille Emana and Samuel Eto'o scored in the space of two minutes.

Star striker Eto'o, a 2009 European Champions League winner with Barcelona, netted decisive goals against Gabon and then against Morocco in the final qualifier to ensure Cameroon topped the group.

Eto'o also set up a spectacular second goal in the 3-0 home win over Togo, dribbling past four defenders before sliding a pass for Jean Makoun to tuck away.

Former Cameroon forward Patrick Mboma believes his country now has a core of very good players but Le Guen has made two important decisions. He transferred the captaincy from veteran defender Rigobert Song to Eto'o. The second was to recall Mallorca striker Webo to the national squad and both have delivered for him.

He also put his trust in Alex Song to patrol

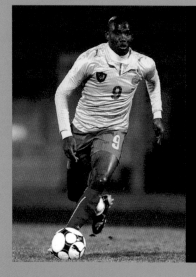

STAR PLAYER

SAMUEL ETO'O
Born: March 10, 1981, Douala • **Club:** Internazionale (Italy)

Eto'o qualifies as one of the greats of African soccer having been voted African Player of the Year three times and is the leading scorer in African Nations Cup history. South Africa will be the powerful striker's third appearance at the World Cup finals having made his debut at France 1998 aged 17. He shot Cameroon to soccer gold at the Sydney 2000 Olympics and has scored more than 40 goals for his country since. His powerful play has also helped Barcelona win the European Champions League twice and he netted more than 100 league goals for them. He joined Internazionale in the summer of 2009, in a part-exchange for Zlatan Ibrahimovic.

ONES TO WATCH

IDRISS KAMENI
Born: February 18, 1984 • **Club:** Espanyol (Spain)

After representing his country since he was 16 Cameroon's acrobatic goalkeeper has won more than 50 caps. He became the youngest soccer player to win an Olympic gold medal when, at 16, he starred in Cameroon's victory at Sydney. His club career stalled at Le Havre in France where he got only three starts but he moved to Espanyol in 2004 where he has quickly established himself as first-choice goalkeeper.

ALEX SONG
Born: September 9, 1987 • **Club:** Arsenal (England)

The canny eye of Arsenal's manager Arsene Wenger spotted the potential in this defensive midfielder. Song, nephew of Rigobert, had already established himself as a 17-year-old in the Bastia side when Wenger signed him. He is now an integral part of the Arsenal and Cameroon set-ups. He made his international debut in the 2008 African Nations Cup

the space in front of the back four, an anchor role he excels in at Arsenal in England. Song's hard work has become a crucial element in Le Guen's formation.

Observers put the win over Gabon as the turning point when the team shed its lackadaisical tendency of their early-qualification performances and Le Guen at last knew he had instilled a strong work ethic.

Their South Africa appearance will be Cameroon's sixth in the finals – a record for an African country. They have missed out only once since 1990 when Pierre Wome's penalty miss against Egypt cost them a place at Germany 2006.

Le Guen is working to better Cameroon's elimination at the group stages in the 1994, 1998 and 2002 World Cups finals. They won Olympic soccer gold in 2000 and remain a major power in Africa.

Many Cameroonians have become global names in soccer – midfielder Marc-Vivien Foe, goalkeeper Jacques Songo'o and Eto'o among them.

Rigobert Song will be 34 during the finals but remains a commanding figure in defence and former Real Madrid and Chelsea midfielder Geremi adds considerable experience.

Goalkeeper Idriss Kameni is a battle-hardened veteran and defenders Sebastien Bassong and Benoit Assou-Ekotto are both English Premiership regulars. Eto'o, Makoun and Webo provide the attacking threat.

The youth element coming through the squad is Alex Song, covering defender Nicolas Nkoulou and midfielder Joel Nguemo.

When they start their campaign in South Africa the Cameroon team will be psyched up by the memories of Italia 90 and the legend of their hero Milla who set a World Cup standard for them to emulate.

MAN IN CHARGE

PAUL LE GUEN

Le Guen took over the Cameroon team as late as July 2009, initially on a short-term contract, and quickly restored a work ethic to a jaded squad. Transforming their qualifying campaign after a poor start has also resurrected his own coaching career. Although he made his name at Rennes developing young stars from Africa, Le Guen has had a chequered career of highs and lows. He took Lyon to three successive French titles and the Champions League quarter-finals but has never shied from making controversial decisions – which led him to a speedy exit after seven months at Glasgow Rangers. He later rescued Paris Saint-German from relegation – but was sacked for inconsistent league form, despite their cup successes.

Group F

ITALY

Inconsistent form for World Cup holders Italy continues to engender a love-hate relationship with their critical supporters but they still go to South Africa bidding for a fifth World Cup championship.

Although they qualified comfortably for South Africa, a series of jaded performances since and a disastrous Confederations Cup campaign in 2009 have raised questions about Italy's ability to win the World Cup for a second consecutive time.

Fans have been furious with some of the team's performances in qualifying, particularly against minnows and are questioning the durability of an ageing squad.

Coach Marcello Lippi has backed his squad which contains many of the players who beat France in a controversial final in 2006. He believes his team is one for the big occasions such as the South Africa finals; never shining in qualifying.

He, too, has a love-hate relationship with Italy's fanatical and vociferous support. They worry about stuttering displays while Lippi, who steered Italy to its 2006 success, tells them to wait and see. He is confident that in the five or six weeks of the finals in South Africa "everything will be different."

After masterminding Italy's fourth World Cup triumph he retired but bowed to popular pressure to replace Roberto Donadoni whose side were eliminated by Spain in the Euro 2008 quarter-finals.

Lippi has retained the core of the 2006 team. World Cup medal holders Gianluigi Buffon, Gianluca Zambrotta, Fabio Grosso, Daniele De Rossi, Andrea Pirlo, Mauro Camoranesi and Vincenzo Iaquinta all started against the Republic of Ireland when Italy sealed qualification with a draw. So did Alberto Gilardino, who scored Italy's late equaliser.

The game that really got the Italian fan base steamed up was when Lippi fielded his second string against Cyprus in Italy's final game. Fans' frustration boiled over when Cyprus took a 2-0 lead and they were not placated by Gilardino replying with a match-winning hat-trick.

An angry Lippi cited Italy's unbeaten seven wins and three draws and accused critics of "lacking respect."

In the uncertain displays along the route to qualification Italy needed a Antonio De Natale's

STAR PLAYER

GIANLUIGI BUFFON
Born: January 28, 1978, Carrara • **Club:** Juventus (Italy)

Bravery and acrobatic skills might be some of Buffon's attributes but so is loyalty. When Juventus, the club which paid a world record £32m for him, were relegated to Serie B in 2006 after a betting scandal, Buffon could have taken his pick of new clubs after starring in Italy's World Cup victory. He chose to stay and helped them regain their Serie A status. Buffon has been Italy's number one since 1997 and is rated among the world's top keepers. He needed knee surgery after Italy qualified for South Africa but is expected to be at his best again by summer 2010. With Juventus he won two league titles with them and played in the 2003 European Cup final.

ONES TO WATCH

FABIO CANNAVARO
Born: September 13, 1973 • **Club:** Juventus (Italy)

Centre-back Cannavaro was voted FIFA World Player of the Year after he skippered Italy to World Cup victory in 2006. At 32, he was the oldest player to win the award. He holds Italy's all-time caps record, having surpassed Paolo Maldini's total of 126 against Switzerland in 2009. He says he is considering retirement if he lifts the World Cup again in 2010.

DANIELE DE ROSSI
Born: July 24, 1983 • **Club:** Roma (Italy)

What a difference four years make. De Rossi has gone from a substitute in the 2006 World Cup final, to one of Lippi's key players for 2010. The midfielder is a tough tackler and energetically covers a lot of ground during a match. With Gattuso in the Italy team De Rossi gets the freedom to go more forward than the defensive role he plays for his club Roma, but he has a powerful shot and recently hit a spectacular 30-yarder against Georgia.

stoppage-time strike to win their opening game in Cyprus; they were lethargic in a 2-1 home win over Montenegro and only won 2-0 in Georgia thanks to two Kakha Kaladze own goals.

Then came Italy's embarrassing Confederations Cup trip to South Africa. A 3-1 win over 10-man United States was followed by a 1-0 defeat to African champions Egypt.

Lippi wrote it off as "one of those games" but his players failed him again when Italy's 3-0 defeat by Brazil sent them home early. The result was even more angry headlines in the lively and often-unforgiving Italian sports' media.

Italy is going through a trough in youth development where the young talent has slowed to a trickle. Unfortunately 10 of the squad for the final qualifiers were over 30. Only two – teenage defender Davide Santon and US-born striker Giuseppe Rossi – were under 25.

Lippi does have the option to experiment with under-21 stars such as midfielders Sebastian Giovinco and Claudio Marchisio plus strikers Roberto Acquafresca and Mario Balotelli in the warm-up games prior to South Africa.

The indications are that Lippi's veterans will be sent in to try to take that fifth championship for their country. Buffon has been voted one of the world's great keepers and in front of him is a formidable defence, organised around the Azzurri's record international Cannavaro.

Andrea Pirlo and the dynamic Daniele De Rossi can drive the midfield but Lippi would like a settled strike force. His options include Iaquinta, Gilardino, Fabio Quagliarella, Giampaolo Pazzini, De Natale and Rossi who all had a chance to shine during the qualifiers. Lippi and his squad may not always see eye to eye with their supporters over the manner of winning but share with the Italian public that the most important thing is to win.

MAN IN CHARGE

MARCELLO LIPPI

Even without masterminding Italy's last World Cup-winning campaign, Lippi is one of the most successful coaches of the modern era. The only man to have led European Champions Cup winners (Juventus 1996) and World Cup winners says the latter in 2006 was his most satisfying moment. His club CV is also very impressive. He took charge at Juventus in 1994 and led them to the Serie A title in his first season, then steered them to two more championships and European Cup finals in 1997 and 1998. He had no success at Inter Milan but on his return to his spiritual home at Juventus they won two further titles and reached another European Cup final in 2003.

PARAGUAY

Paraguay hope a change of image will help the country past the last 16 at the World Cup for the first time. Long admired for being well-organised defensively, they are aiming for a quarter-finals place thanks to a trio of gifted forwards.

Attacking flair took Paraguay to their fourth successive World Cup finals from their South America qualifying group with two games to spare but, having not got past the second round in 1986, 1998, 2002 and 2006, they are hoping the new attack formula will do it for them.

Traditionally solid defensively, Paraguay now has the combined firepower of Roque Santa Cruz, Nelson Haedo Valdez and Salvador Cabanas up front.

And taking the scalp of much-vaunted Argentina in qualifying, thanks to Valdez's winner, was no mean feat and testament to the all-round talent across the team. Valdez stunned Argentina with a left-foot shot after a slick move involving Cabanas twisting clear of two defenders and playing a one-two with midfielder Edgar Barreto.

Optimism is high among the Paraguayan squad because they qualified despite the frequent absence of Manchester City's Santa Cruz who started only five matches because of recurrent knee trouble. Coach Gerardo Martino likened it to Argentina having to do without Messi or Brazil without Kaka.

Santa Cruz has meant a lot to the team since he made his international debut aged only 17. For Martino a Santa Cruz, Valdez and Cabanas combination is a must for South Africa 2010. He points to the way the threesome tormented the Brazilian defence in Paraguay's 2-0 win in Asuncion as Paraguay made a flying start to their campaign then went on to win seven and draw two of their opening 10 games.

Qualification was not without its hiccups. Without their talisman Santa Cruz on each occasion they suffered an early 4-2 defeat to Bolivia at altitude in La Paz; were defeated 2-0 in Uruguay; and needed an Edgar Benitez 92nd minute equaliser to rescue a point in Ecuador.

With Santa Cruz they also slumped 2-0 at home to Chile and lost 2-1 in Brazil.

Paraguay came back on track for South Africa

STAR PLAYER

NELSON HAEDO VALDEZ
Born: November 28, 1983 • **Club:** Borussia Dortmund (Germany)

Valdez, as a homeless teenager, used to sleep rough under the terraces at Paraguay's Tembetary stadium, but now wows thousands of fans sitting on them. Quick, technically gifted and with an eye for goal he is now one of Paraguay's biggest stars with more than 50 caps. He netted five times in the qualifying campaign. His international career was a bit of a gamble as he was called into Paraguay's squad for the 2003 Under-20 World Cup finals even though the coaches had hardly seen him play. They did not have to worry about his abilities and he was quickly in the senior team. He understudied, and learned from, Germany's Miroslav Klose and Croatia's Ivan Klasnic at Werder Bremen and has become a national team regular since joining Borussia Dortmund in 2006.

ONES TO WATCH

SALVADOR CABANAS

Born: August 5, 1980 • **Club:** Club America (Mexico)

The 2007 South American Player of the Year led Paraguay's scorers with six goals in qualifying and is regarded as the most versatile of Paraguay's attackers because he can play up front; out wide; or drop deep to create goal opportunities for others. Cabanas is a prolific scorer in Mexican soccer with more than 100 goals.

ROQUE SANTA CRUZ

Born: August 16, 1981 • **Club:** Manchester City (England)

Santa Cruz is one of the players in South Africa whom all Paraguay prays will stay clear of injuries. Suspect knees reduced his games in qualifying and as the focal point of Paraguay's attack he is vital. The big striker is not only outstanding in the air and possesses a poacher's instinct in the box but he can hold the ball up and bring colleagues into play.

Dario Veron who is with Universidad Nacional in the same league.

Paraguayans say their country has never entered a World Cup finals with a stronger squad. Optimism is high for a squad that is not among the bookmakers' favourites but have a lethal enough strike force to be rated dangerous outsiders, capable of springing a shock – or two.

with a decisive Cabanas penalty against Bolivia and the victory over Argentina.

Previous unsuccessful Paraguay World Cup campaigns may have been long forgotten although not their extrovert goalkeeper Jose Luis Chilavert of 1998 and 2002 fame who took penalties.

The current crop of players believe they can eradicate the bitter memories of the under-achievement of going out at the first hurdle at Germany 2006 because there is a far greater team spirit now.

Valdez is among several of the present squad returning with another chance to make good last time's elimination at the group stage after losing to England and Sweden. He says: "It's a chance to do better."

The Paraguayan squad members play all over the world absorbing experience from some top clubs. 70-cap goalkeeper Justo Villar, plays in Spain with Valldolid while defenders Caceres and Claudio Morel are with top Argentine club Boca Juniors. Barreto is in Italy's Serie A for Atalanta and striker Oscar Cardozo joined Benfica in Portugal in 2009. Midfielder Cristian Riveros is with Mexican side Cruz Azul and often faces defender

MAN IN CHARGE

GERARDO MARTINO

Martino has had a huge influence on Paraguayan soccer for nearly a decade at club and international levels. His success with Cerro Porteno and Club Libertad made him the obvious candidate to succeed Anibal Ruiz as national coach in 2007. He has nurtured probably the most gifted Paraguay squad for years through the roller coaster of qualifying. He has succeeded in being a calming influence when the pressure was on the team. He now has at his command a group of experienced players at their peak and many believe there will never be a better opportunity for a Paraguay side to go further in the finals than ever before. Their Argentine-born coach is being optimistically cautious and says the soccer-loving public should not get ahead of themselves. He has been quoted as saying: "There are two things you can aim for as a coach – to get results, or go down in history. I'm after the latter."

Group F

NEW ZEALAND

The New Zealand team has a lot to prove in South Africa. Their soccer players – dubbed the All Whites – have to break out of the shadow of their illustrious rugby union and cricket brethren to break their duck in a World Cup finals.

Soccer is certainly on the up in New Zealand as proved by a record crowd of 35,000 packing the West-Pac Stadium in Wellington to cheer the team to 1-0 victory over Bahrain that clinched the Oceana region as champions – and their ticket to the World Cup finals of 2010.

After years of competing with cricket and rugby for public attention New Zealand soccer players have reached the World Cup finals for only the second time – and this time they will want to pick some points.

In Spain in 1982 at their last World Cup appearance they were ignominiously eliminated at the group stage after losing to Scotland, the Soviet Union and Brazil.

New Zealand coach Ricki Herbert and his assistant Brian Turner both played in that campaign and know that it will not be an easy task to erase the memories of defeat in 1982.

New Zeland have recently sampled playing conditions in South Africa although not positively. In the 2009 Confederations Cup they lost 5-0 to Spain, 2-0 to South Africa and drew 0-0 with Iraq.

Yet captain Ryan Nelsen believes those experiences aided them in their final qualifiers. He said there were harsh lessons from the Spain and South Africa defeats they can absorb in preparation for summer 2010.

With old rivals Australia opting to go for successful qualification via the Asian Confederation route, New Zealand were excused Oceana pre-qualifying. They easily topped the group with five wins out of six then the play-offs against fifth-placed Asian side Bahrain.

After drawing 0-0 in Bahrain, thanks to Mark Paston's goalkeeping heroics, Rory Fallon sent the All-Whites through by heading the winning goal in the return.

Coach Herbert said the strong belief running through his side was a key factor in reaching the finals and Nelsen believes it will be a springboard for the growth of soccer among rugby-mad Kiwis. Fallon also believes the dark days for New Zealand soccer are over with this achievement.

STAR PLAYER

RYAN NELSEN
Born: October 18, 1977 • **Club:** Blackburn Rovers (England)

Centre back Nelsen is the man New Zealand's players look to for inspiration. Commanding in the back line he is the leader and organiser of the side, as he calmly showed under pressure in the closing stages against Bahrain. He is also arguably the country's most successful soccer export and has had a globetrotting career. He left New Zealand in 1997 to play college soccer in the United States before making his name with Washington club DC United. He was twice named in Major League Soccer's "Team of the Season" before joining Blackburn five years ago to become an English Premiership regular and club captain. Injuries and club commitments restricted his international appearances from 2004-08, but he returned to be a key figure in New Zealand's qualifying campaign.

ONES TO WATCH

RORY FALLON
Born: March 20, 1982 • **Club:** Plymouth Argyle (England)

Fallon went from new boy to hero when his decisive goal went in against against Bahrain. For the son of Kevin Fallon, assistant New Zealand coach at the1982 World Cup finals, it was his second strike in only his third New Zealand appearance. He had only in June 2009 became eligible for the country of his birth after a FIFA rule change because he had chosen to play for England at youth level.

MARK PASTON
Born: December 13, 1976 • **Club:** Wellington Phoenix

Paston gets a huge amount of credit for New Zealand reaching the South Africa finals. In the away leg of the play-off against Bahrain he stepped in for suspended regular goalkeeper keeper Glen Moss and made a succession of saves in the 0-0 draw. In the return in Wellington he pulled off a vital penalty save. His reward? A highly-publicised kiss from Herbert after the final whistle and a stronger claim to a regular spot in the team.

The same 18-man squad which successfully saw New Zealand through both games against Bahrain is likely to form the core of Herbert's World Cup party.

The New Zealanders of 1982 were all part-timers and the country still lacks a professional league although more New Zealand-grown stars are making an impact in leagues around the world. The 1982 debacle launched the career of striker Wynton Rufer, who starred with Werder Bremen in the German Bundesliga, while of the current cop of Kiwi internationals Nelsen is a star of the Blackburn Rovers' defence in the English Premier League.

Wellington Phoenix is the country's only full-time professional club but they compete – with Paston, international defenders Ben Sigmund, Tony Lochhead and David Mulligan and midfielder Leo Bertos – in Australia's A-League.

New Zealand's most-capped player, defender Ivan Vicelich, still plays only part-time for Auckland City while midfielder Simon Elliott is withSan Jose Earthquakes in the United States.

Fallon plays for English Championship side Plymouth Argyle where he competes with teenage striker Chris Woods at West Bromwich Albion. Forward Chris Killen plies his trade with Celtic in Scotland.

Shane Smeltz, who led the Oceana group scoring list with eight goals, turns out in the A-League as does midfielder Michael McGlinchey.

Tactical changes may be required by Herbert when he faces the world's elite in South Africa. His favoured 3-4-3 formation of the play-offs may have to be sacrificed to reinforce his defence when the opposition gets stronger.

MAN IN CHARGE

RICKI HERBERT

Herbert has celebrated a decade long association with the New Zealand national side and he has been a "Jack-of-all-trades." In 1999 he took charge of the country's Olympic hopefuls but he has also been under-17 coach, national technical director and assistant to previous All-Whites coach Mick Waitt. He took over from Waitt in 2005 and steered New Zealand to victory in the Oceana Nations Cup three years later. Herbert is fairly unique in that he has reached the World Cup finals as a player and coach. As a 21-year-old defender he appeared in the 1982 finals, starting against the Soviet Union and Brazil. He later played in Australia and had a spell in England with Wolverhampton Wanderers. He is still involved with club soccer as he combines the role of national coach with manager of Wellington Phoenix.

SLOVAKIA

A big dose of irony will be behind Slovakia's first-ever visit to the World Cup finals. The surprise package of European qualifying Group Three had to dispose of neighbours the Czech Republic of whom they were part until 1993.

After three failed attempts to qualify Slovakia has the chance to come out of the shadow of the Czech Republic which has a more illustrious soccer heritage as consistent World Cup performers and were runners-up at Euro 96 and semi finalists at Euro 2004.

Although Slovakia's 1-0 away win in a blizzard in Poland sealed their entry to their first major finals, the group qualifying games against the much-fancied Czech Republic delighted Slovak fans even more.

Slovakia won the "derby" qualifier 2-1 in the Czech capital Prague then battled with 10 men to a home 2-2 draw in Bratislava.

Pessimism over Slovakia's chances of making South Africa had grown with stalwart Marek Mintal quitting international soccer to concentrate on his club career with Nurnberg in Germany.

Captain Robert Vittek led by example the "hungry young men" of Slovakia who were not expected to do as well as they did given that were drawn in what looked to be one of the toughest European groups. He has pledged to take that hunger to South Africa.

The qualifying path to South Africa was not easy. A surprise 2-0 home defeat by Slovenia meant it was vital to win their final game with four regulars, including top scorer Stanislav Sestak missing through suspension, against Poland.

Poland's Severyn Gancarczyk helped Slovakia out inside three minutes when he turned a cross into his own net. Slovakia goalkeeper Jan Mucha produced a series of saves to preserve the points.

Since his appointment in 2008 national coach Vladimir Weiss, a former Czechoslovakia international as a player, has been blooding young players from the burgeoning Slovakian national league and youth programmes.

Major soccer exports from Slovakia have been centre back Martin Skrtel to English Premier League and Champions League contenders Liverpool and full back Marek Cech to England's West Bromwich Albion. Weiss' son, also Vladimir,

STAR PLAYER

STANISLAV SESTAK
Born: December 16, 1982 • **Club:** Bochum (Germany)

Sestak led Slovakia's scorers in qualifying with six goals in as many appearances and some of them were vital match winners. A move to Germany's Bundesliga in 2007 has been seen as the reason behind his more-seasoned and sharper play. Sestak's reputation has grown steadily and he is something of a talisman with the national squad because he was never on the losing side in qualifying. He scored twice in three minutes to overturn Poland's 1-0 lead and kick start his team's campaign, then he turned a tricky fixture in Northern Ireland with a 15th-minute goal. He also netted in each "derby" game against the Czech Republic and national coach Weiss will look to Sestak for not only goals but also coolness on the pitch.

ONES TO WATCH

MARTIN SKRTEL
Born: December 15, 1984 • **Club:** Liverpool (England)

Slovakia looks to Skrtel for experience as the only Slovak with regular Champions' League experience. The battle-hardened Liverpool defender is the cornerstone of Slovakia's back line – but he was a striker. The switch came when the 16-year-old filled in at centre back for the Slovak youth team. He made such a good job of it, it has been his role ever since. He is strong in the air and is a threat at corners and free kicks.

JAN MUCHA
Born: December 5, 1982 • **Club:** Legia Warsaw (Poland)

The confidence of the Slovakia team has grown with their goalkeeper Mucha. Weiss promoted him for the Czech Republic qualifier in Prague and Mucha repaid the coach with an excellent display in Slovakia's win. The agile shot stopper was also outstanding in the away wins over Northern Ireland and Poland which saw his team through to the finals.

is with Manchester City while Miroslav Stoch is signed to Chelsea.

Elsewhere in Europe, defensive midfielder Miroslav Karhan, the most capped of all Slovak players, has been playing in Germany for nine years. Hamsik is with Napoli and striker Filip Holosko with Besiktas of Istanbul.

Coach Weiss has built resilience into Slovakia's game. They came from a goal down with seven minutes left to beat Poland 2-1 in Bratislava, and needed all their nerve to win over the Czechs and beat off Northern Ireland's tough challenge in Belfast.

A 2-1 home defeat by fellow qualifiers Chile in a World Cup warm-up friendly means there are still aspects of the Slovakia game that need improvement. Questions to be answered are getting more support for Sestak, who was the leading scorer in qualifying, and how to perform well when Hamsik is shackled in midfield the way he was against Chile.

The Slovakian media has questioned how the young defender Peter Pekarik, and midfielders Weiss Junior and Stoch will cope with the inevitable pressure in South Africa. Veteran Zdenko Strba may need all his nous to hold the midfield

together at the very high level demanded by the World Cup finals.

Depletion of the team through indiscipline presents another problem for Weiss Senior. He had Roman Kratochvil sent off in San Marino; Hasik dismissed against the Czechs in Bratislava; while Skrtel, Zabavnik, Stoch and Jan Durica were banned for the trip to Poland.

89

MAN IN CHARGE

VLADIMIR WEISS
International soccer is literally in the blood for the Slovakia coach – three generations of it. He leads his squad into the World Cup finals 20 years after he played for the old Czechoslovakia at Italia 1990. As an Inter Bratislava midfielder Weiss won 19 caps for Czechoslovakia and 12 for Slovakia. His father, also Vladimir, but a centre back, started the family heritage in soccer when he gained three caps for Czechoslovakia. Coming up to date, Weiss' son, another Vladimir, is a an integral part of the current Slovakia squad. Weiss' coaching skills came to the notice of the Slovakian FA when he guided Artmedia into the 2005 European Champions' League. It put Weiss in the frame to succeed Jan Kocian in 2008. With the national squad Weiss' psychology has been to put an emphasis on organisation and team spirit and as a result they have responded to overthrow the tag of underdogs.

BRAZIL

It is hard to believe that the undoubted World Cup kings Brazil, the only nation to have competed in every finals tournament and won it a record five times, should be booed off the field.

That day was June 18, 2008, when Brazil failed to sparkle in a 0-0 draw with Argentina in a World Cup qualifier and three days earlier had lost 2-0 in Paraguay. In the media national coach of two years Dunga was pictured with his head in a noose and a national newspaper editorialised: "The future looks bleak".

But this is a Brazilian national team and they don't stay in the doldrums for long. Just over a year later they had blown away the newspaper headlines calling them "donkeys" by being the first team to qualify from the South American group – with three games to spare.

Even more satisfying for national pride was that they had beaten bitter rivals Argentina 3-1. Inspirational captain Lucio said it showed the Brazilian squad could handle the pressure.

National expectations of a comfortable World Cup qualification began to form when a depleted Brazil side had beaten favourites Argentina 3-0 in the 2007 Copa America final.

But the fates had conspired against Brazil who struggled after losing inspirational Kaka for 11 months to a string of injuries. This came at a time when Dunga, a former midfield general with the national side, was trying not only to implement a winning pattern but also getting the players to make it work.

Kaka proved his talismanic status on his return and inspired the team to a 0-0 draw against Colombia. Sevilla striker Luis Fabiano proved that Brazil were not a team with only one star performer by netting nine goals during qualification, including two against Argentina.

Dunga shook up the defence, too, and discovered a new centre back in Luisao to partner Lucio. He also added left back Andre Santos, to cement a new backbone to the team.

Brazil then really clicked and qualified in style with a 3-0 win over Peru, 4-0 in Uruguay, 2-1 against Paraguay, then Argentina. The team responded to Dunga's exhortations not to relax and, four days

STAR PLAYER

KAKA (Ricardo Izecson dos Santos Leite)
Born: April 22, 1982 • **Club:** Real Madrid (Spain)

His return to the Brazil team, after months of niggling injuries, gave the boost they needed to clinch early qualification. Brazil had won just one of five matches in his absence. Kaka starred against Argentina in Rosario. He tee-ed up the second goal with a deft pass to Gilberto, then split the home defence for Luis Fabiano to score the third. While very much the playmaker for Brazil, Kaka has other skills on the pitch such as being able to glide past opponents and score from long range. Kaka survived a spinal fracture sustained in a swimming pool accident at 18 to become, albeit briefly, a world record transfer from Milan to Real Madrid. The price for buying one of the greats of modern soccer, and 2007's World Player of the Year, was £68.5million.

ONES TO WATCH

LUCIO (Lucimar Ferreira da Silva)
Born: May 8, 1978 • **Club:** Internazionale (Italy)

Already a World Cup winner from 2002, Lucio is Dunga's lieutenant on the pitch. The vastly-experienced captain is a vigilant marker and leader of Brazil's solid back line. There is an excellence to all aspects of his game from being outstanding in the air and a perpetual danger as the target for free kicks and corners to his remarkable ability to tackle without collecting yellow cards.

ROBINHO (Robson de Souza)
Born: January 25, 1984 • **Club:** Manchester City (England)

Mobile winger Robinho works best playing off a lead striker and has forged a superb Brazilian goal-scoring partnership with Luis Fabiano. He has a less-profitable time with his club Manchester City in the English Premier League's physical environment where he battles to justify his British record fee of £32m. Always a threat for Brazil, he has scored consistently in more than 70 appearances.

after that win in Argentina, Nilmar scored a hat-trick as Brazil beat Chile 4-2.

Traditionalists, who hanker for the flair sides that featured Pele, Garrincha and Ronaldo over the years, may not agree with Dunga's emphasis on defence and discipline. His advice before the team went out in Rosario against Argentina was that winning depended on overcoming provocation in such a tense match and keeping 11 men on the pitch.

The qualifying statistics back Dunga's policy of stiffening the defence; Brazil conceded only seven goals in their first 15 qualifiers with goalkeeper Julio Cesar, looking the best in that position for several decades since Gilmar 50 years ago. He was outstanding in the 1-1 draw with Ecuador and again against Uruguay.

Lucio and Maicon have developed an understanding born of playing together at Inter Milan and are a formidable presence.

Brazil sports two defensive midfielders, the experienced ex-Arsenal man Gilberto from the 2002 World Cup winning side and Felipe Melo of Juventus.

This give the attackers Kaka, Elano and Robinho the freedom to roam dangerously and Luis Fabiano proved himself the natural successor to Ronaldo and Adriano with two goals which turned the 2009 Confederations Cup final in South Africa from being a real shocker for the Brazilian nation. Luis Fabiano struck after the United States roared into a 2-0 lead inside 30 minutes and Lucio headed the winner as Brazil recovered to win 3-2.

The doubters of 2008 were shown both the flair and the resilience that make Brazil one of the favourites to triumph again in South Africa.

MAN IN CHARGE

DUNGA (Carlos Caetano Bledorn Verri)
A dignified silence to the early critics of his regime and methods as national coach has proved the best strategy for Dunga – he let his team do the talking on the pitch. His was a controversial appointment when he succeeded Carlos Alberto Parreira in 2006. The 1994 World Cup-winning captain had never coached a professional team before, the critics moaned and they slammed his single-minded approach and his emphasis on power and physical preparation. Dunga's philosophy was: "We have obligations. First, to win; second, to score lots of goals; and, third, to put on a show." Critics ate their words as Brazil managed all three to qualify early – without Ronaldo, Ronaldinho or Adriano.

Group G

NORTH KOREA

North Korea stole many of the main headlines 44 years ago when the curtain of Asian communism was briefly drawn back at the 1966 World Cup to reveal a plucky side which won many hearts. They try again in South Africa.

Political controversy is never far away whenever the North Korea national team plays. So it was in the qualifying campaign for South Africa 2010.

The planet's only remaining Stalinist state – virtually sealed from the outside world for decades – drew great regional rivals South Korea in their World Cup qualifying group. Antipathy and politics inevitably reared their ugly heads with a game having to be played on a neutral ground in the spirit of compromise.

North Korea had told the South it could play in the North's capital Pyongyang but the South objected that its national anthem would not be played. The North threatened to boycott the game but eventually a compromise was reached and North Korea's "home" pre-qualifying and final group games against South Korea were switched to the Chinese city of Shanghai.

With a goalless draw in Saudi Arabia North Korea qualified for the World Cup finals for the first time since 1966 on goal difference and as group runners-up to South Korea.

Once qualified, the country's "Great Leader" Kim Il-Sung was said to have personally involved himself with guidance on the development of North Korean soccer and proposed the tactics most relevant for the physiques of the country's players.

The rallying cry for North Korea's players in South Africa will be: "Please the leader and bring fame to the Fatherland."

North Korea's 1966 heroics in England have become the stuff of legend. They beat much-fancied Italy to reach the quarter-finals with Pak Do-ik hitting the only goal in the 42nd minute to send the Italians home in national disgrace.

The North Koreans then led the Portuguese 3-0 before the great Eusebio netted four to steer his team to a 5-3 victory. North Korea has not qualified since partly through sour grapes.

92

STAR PLAYER

JONG TAE-SE
Born: March 2, 1984 • **Club:** Kawaski Frontale (Japan)

On the face of it Jong has a bulldozer style as a striker but that would be to ignore his other attributes upfront – pace, skill and finishing ability. By being born in Japan to a Korean family, he was entitled to South Korean citizenship and, but for his choice to live in the north of Korea, he might have being a regular in capitalist South Korea's national squad and playing professionally in the South's K-League. In interviews he says he wants to do neither of these things as he attended a school in Japan which was partially funded by North Korea and feels he owes his allegiance to the North. Jong is known as "The Bulldozer" because of his physical style but he scored only once in North Korea's final qualifying group. Ironically praise for Jong has come from an unusual source, South Korea coach Huh Jung-moo, who believes he might make an impact at the World Cup.

ONES TO WATCH

AN YOUNG-HAK
Born: October 25, 1978 • **Club:** Suwon Bluewings (South Korea)

Defensive midfielder An is the only North Korean star to play in South Korea's K-League but his experience there may help his team in South Africa. He is another Korean who was born in Japan and he began playing in the Japanese J. League. An is a determined and disciplined marker who is also recognised as a motivator.

HONG YONG-JO
Born: May 22, 1982 • **Club:** FC Rostov (Russia)

The team's dead-ball expert, and captain through the qualifiers, was one of 15 candidates for the Asian Footballer of the Year award in 2009. A clever attacking midfielder who plies his trade at the Rostov club in Russia, he has won more than 40 caps and is the only North Korean with significant European experience.

After their defeat by South Korea in the 1994 qualifiers – the North refused to enter the qualifying for the 1998 and 2002 World Cups.

This time around North Korean coach Kim Jong-hun and his squad started their qualifying campaign with a 4-1 win over Mongolia.

In Shanghai, the North had the better of a 1-1 draw, but Hong Yong-jo's penalty for them was levelled by South Korea's Ki Sung Yeung.

Although they play on the counter, goals were hard to come by for North Korea – just seven in eight games. They rely on star striker Jong Tae-se's quick breaks and the cultured midfield play of Hong Yong-jo.

The veteran midfielder Mun In-guk hit the winner against Saudi Arabia and his 93rd-minute effort in the 2-0 win over United Arab Emirates crucially boosted North Korea's goal difference.

North Korea's defence has been its strength – conceding only five goals. Goalkeeper Ri Myong-guk was outstanding against Saudi Arabia and Iran and his undestanding with formidable defenders Cha Jong-hyok, Ri Jun-il, Ri Kwang-chon and Ji Yun-nam is a key part of the team's success.

North Korea may be cut off politically in the world but not from soccer's global strategies. 10-man North Korea held out for a 0-0 draw in Riyadh, in stifling heat, because astute coach Kim Jong-Hun had spotted the Saudis lack of prolific strikers and so focused on defending.

That is also an indication of his South Africa game plan – deploying a defensive strategy but unleashing Hong Yong-jo and Jong Tae-se to catch out opponents with speed in attack.

It is not a strategy that 1966 hero Pak Do-ik is convinced about. He wants the strength in defence supplemented by the creation of more scoring chances.

93

MAN IN CHARGE

KIM JONG-HUN
Kim is known as a meticulous planner and can put out a team which can frustrate. He takes no chances of the opposition springing a surprise on his team and favours a highly defensive 5-4-1 formation, with a sweeper and two centre backs. In Kim's game plans the full backs rarely attack and the defence is shielded by two midfield anchors. The attacking is done by Hong Yong-jo and Mun In-guk in support of lead striker Jong Tae-Se. Kim explains: "We want to maximize our organisation."

IVORY COAST

Along with the hosts South Africa, Ivory Coast's squad believes success would make a statement for not only their country but also herald the true emergence of Africa in world soccer.

Of all the participants, eyes will be particularly on Chelsea top scorer and Ivory Coast star striker Didier Drogba who would feature in any World XI.

He reckons his side can leave their mark on the history of Ivorian soccer with good performances against the likes of great teams such as Brazil, Italy and Germany.

Drogba says it is important for the squad to make their country proud with at least an appearance in the final. He believes it would change the stereotypes and the way the rest of the world thinks about Africa and African soccer.

It is the Ivory Coast's second consecutive qualification for the World Cup finals but the group draw for Germany 2006 did the Ivorians no favours at all.

They were pitched into a group with such world soccer powers as Argentina and the Netherlands. Despite Drogba scoring the Ivory Coast's first-ever finals' goal, they lost 2-1 to Argentina and Holland.

Ivorian resilience showed itself when they beat Serbia and Montenegro 3-2 after trailing 2-0. Midfielder Yaya Toure says Ivory Coast was unlucky to be in such a tough group but believes the experience will stand them in good stead in South Africa.

Ivory Coast's Bosnian coach Vahid Halilhodzic has also pledged to the west African nation that this time the culmination of the 2010 World Cup is going to be better.

Halilhodzic's style of play is not above criticism and his optimism is not supported by Jean-Marc Guillou of the ASEC Mimosas Academy which has produced a succession of African stars for European clubs. The man who exported the talents of Didier Zokora and brothers Kolo and Yaya Toure says Halilhodzic relies too much on the individual flair and brilliance of players such as Drogba.

Guillou complains Ivory Coast no longer play so much as a team but as a collection of individuals and predicts the Ivorians will fail to reach the last 16.

STAR PLAYER

DIDIER DROGBA
Born: March 11, 1978 • **Club:** Chelsea (England)

Question marks over his dedication and attitude at club level do not arise when his beloved national team calls Drogba. The team is a cause close to his heart, as his record of more than 40 international goals shows. On form he is one of the most fearsome strikers in world soccer who can terrorise defenders with his physical strength. His weapons are excellence in the air, clinical conversion of half chances and his free-kick expertise. The 2006 African Footballer of the Year was sent off in the 2008 Champions League final and did not appear to enjoy his time at Chelsea during Luiz Felipe Scolari's reign. Drogba made his breakthrough at French side Guingamp in 2003 but it was his impressive scoring record for Marseille which earned him a £24m move to Chelsea.

ONES TO WATCH

YAYA TOURE
Born: May 13, 1983 • **Club:** Barcelona (Spain)

Few players are better equipped for the Ivory Coast's defensive midfield anchor role than Yaya Toure. He is tall, deceptively quick and a strong tackler. Yaya, like older brother Kolo, was a product of the ASEC Mimosas youth academy which has helped many African players to stardom. Yaya joined Barcelona from Monaco in a £6m deal in 2007 and helped them win the Champions' League, the Spanish league title and Spanish Cup "treble" in 2009.

BAKARY KONE
Born: September 17, 1981 • **Club:** Marseille (France)

The current Ivorian Player of the Year in 2009 is, at 1.63m (5ft 4in), one of the smallest international strikers but he is quick, clever and a predator in the penalty box. Like teammates Kolo and Yaya Toure Kone is another product of the ASEC Mimosas youth academy. His form for Nice has since earned him a big-money move to Marseille.

Skipper Drogba is quick to defend Halilhodzic for the way he has quickly adapted to the particular demands of Ivorian soccer. Remembering the 2006 finals, Drogba says the squad learned a great deal from playing against such tough opponents. He revealed that naivity was the problem; the side spent too long watching their opponents and not enough time competing with them. He has singled out the win over Serbia as the turning point and a springboard from which they can launch a credible bid for 2010.

In qualifying for South Africa, the Ivorians eased unbeaten through a preliminary group which included Botswana, Mozambique and Madagascar without an injured and suspended Drogba and injured striking partner Arouna Kone. Ivory Coast started the qualifiers proper with a 5-0 home win against Malawi in which the coach blooded an experimental side. They then won 2-1 in Guinea and 3-2 in Burkina Faso. A home romp against Burkina Faso, this time 5-0, guaranteed their South African ticket with Drogba leading the Ivorian scorers with six goals.

The Ivory Coast has a number of big occasion players. Midfielder

Yaya Toure is a 2009 Champions League winner with Barcelona, while Drogba (Marseille and Chelsea) and defender Kolo Toure (Arsenal and Manchester City) have big-club pedigrees.

Salomon Kalou of Chelsea and Arsenal's Emmanuel Eboue compete at the top of the English Premiership while Romaric starts most weeks for Sevilla. Guy Demel plays for Hamburg in Germany; goalkeeper Boubacar Barry for Lokeren in Belgium; and Kader Keita is a new recruit for Turkey's Galatasaray.

These big-match players now face their biggest matches at international level.

95

MAN IN CHARGE

VAHID HALILHODZIC

Expectations are high in the Ivory Coast that Bosnian coach Halilhodzic will make a success of his first international job, especially in the South Africa finals. However, Halilhodzic is much travelled as a club coach and made his name with French side Lille by taking them from the second division to a Champions' League place in just four years between 1998 and 2002. He also guided Paris Saint-Germain to a league runners-up spot plus the French cup in 2004 then led Al-Ittihad to the Saudi Arabian league title in 2007. He succeeded German Uli Stielike as the Ivory Coast coach in 2008.

PORTUGAL

Portugal is looking to a new "Golden Generation" to succeed where the previous holders of that coveted title have failed – to, at last, win the World Cup.

Portugal's so-called "Golden Generation" of names such as Luis Figo, Rui Costa and Fernando Couto have gone down in world soccer history as "nearly men" as 2006 World Cup semi-finalists and Euro 2004 beaten finalists.

The new generation including Deco and Cristiano Ronaldo are upbeat about their chances in South Africa despite a struggle to qualify. Only 1-0 wins home and away in a play-off against Bosnia got them to the World Cup finals. Coach Carlos Queiroz believes Portugal will be firm contenders to win, or be in the top four, in South Africa.

The key to the success of Portugal's undoubtedly talent-filled squad is the wing play of Ronaldo. When he was not at his best in the qualifiers – neither was the team. But Queiroz is relying on the talents of Real Madrid's £80m forward to attack from any position with pace and power, score with either foot, or his head and rattle in thunderous free kicks. The coach needs Ronaldo free of his recent ankle trouble, consistency from Nani and continuing dynamic performances from Chelsea full-back Jose Bosingwa if Portugal are to make an impact. In Ricardo Carvalho of Chelsea, Real Madrid's Pepe and Porto star Bruno Alves they have battle-hardened veterans in defence with Alves always likely to surge forward to score a goal.

Veteran Chelsea midfielder Deco, like Carvalho, wants a World Cup medal to go with the European Champions League gongs they already possess. Emerging out of midfield with probing runs is winger Simao who combines experience with goals while Raul Meireles, a determined midfield anchor, scored the winner in Bosnia.

The Brazilian effect may tell in Portugal's quest for world domination. Queiroz hopes striker Liedson – Brazilian-born, like Deco and Pepe – will follow in the footsteps of Nuno Gomes and Pauleta before them in putting in superb performances for their adopted country.

Portugal's coach also has younger talents in reserve

STAR PLAYER

CRISTIANO RONALDO
Born: February 5, 1985 • **Club:** Real Madrid (Spain)

Portugal have some big guns to fire in South Africa including Ronaldo, at £85m, the world's most expensive – and arguably – greatest player. He moved from Manchester United to Real Madrid in 2009 after winning the European Champions' League in 2008 and three Premier League titles at Manchester. Although he was Europe's top scorer in 2008, when he was also voted World and European Player of the Year, he has yet fully to shine at international level despite making his Portugal debut at 18 and winning around 70 caps for his country. He was named in UEFA's "Team of the Tournament" when Portugal reached the Euro 2004 final and has since helped Portugal to the 2006 World Cup semi-finals and the quarter-finals of Euro 2008. Queiroz made Ronaldo captain for the qualifiers but he failed to score, before ankle trouble forced him to miss Portugal's last group game and the play-offs.

ONES TO WATCH

RAUL MEIRELES
Born: March 17, 1983 • **Club:** Porto (Portugal)

Meireles is an enforcer and his job is to protect the defence, win the ball, then set his creative colleagues free. Despite not having the explosive qualities of Ronaldo, Deco, Simao or Nani he plays a crucial role for Portugal and was the only player to start all 12 of their qualifiers. He has a powerful long-range shot in his armoury and occasionally breaks to score important goals, none more so than the winner in Bosnia.

LIEDSON
Born: December 17, 1977 (Brazil) • **Club:** Sporting Clube (Portugal)

The Brazil-born striker was granted Portuguese nationality in August 2009 and immediately fast-tracked into the international squad. Nicknamed "Levezinho" (the slender one) because of his light build, he has scored 150-plus goals for Sporting in seven years. His Portugal colleagues breathed a sigh of relief when he scored a match-saving equaliser in Denmark on his debut. He added another in the 3-0 win over Hungary.

to call upon such as Hugo Almeida, Fabio Coentrao, Miguel Veloso and Joao Moutinho.

The vital goalkeeper slot is a straight choice between Braga's Eduardo, who featured largely in the qualifiers, and Benfica's more-experienced Quim.

Queiroz believes that benefits in bonding the squad have emerged from the qualifying struggles. The squad, he said, has developed great solidarity and fighting spirit. Appointed as Portugal's coach in 2008, Queiroz has the spectre of his predecessor Luiz Felipe Scolari hanging over his South African campaign. Having won the World Cup with Brazil, Scolari had set a high precedent by steering Portugal to the 2006 semi-finals and the Euro 2004 final where they were beaten by unfancied Greece.

In qualifying for South Africa 2010 Portugal suffered a shock 3-2 home defeat to Denmark. In an amazing late slump Portugal lost after leading 2-1 with 120 seconds left. Three 0-0 draws followed leaving Portugal needing to win their last three games to qualify.

A 3-0 win at home to Hungary while Sweden lost 1-0 in Denmark was the break Portugal needed before a 4-0 home win over Malta clinched a vital play-off place.

Being the nearly-men in recent soccer history has been a problem for Portugal's international side. They lost 1-0 to France – by just a Zinedine Zidane penalty – in Germany 2006 which had been a repeat of Euro 2000, when Zidane's spot kick settled a bad-tempered semi-final. A greater blow to Portuguese pride was the Euro 2004 final defeat to the tournament's surprise package Greece. Determined not to repeat these bad memories, and that of elimination by Germany in the Euro 2008 quarter-finals, Queiroz, Ronaldo, Deco and co will be keen to lay those ghosts to rest in South Africa.

MAN IN CHARGE

CARLOS QUEIROZ

Queiroz will at last make his first World Cup finals appearance in South Africa – and he was so close once before. Ironically he had coached South Africa to the joint-hosted Japan/South Korea finals 2002, but left before the tournament after a row with the South African soccer authorities. He was in charge of Portugal once before, 1991-93, but quit after they failed to qualify for Euro 92 or the 1994 World Cup. Queiroz had a hand in bringing through Portugal's previous "Golden Generation". He had made his name coaching the under-20s and developing such potential stars as Luis Figo, Rui Costa, Fernando Couto, Joao Pinto and Vitor Baia. At club level, Queiroz had two spells as Sir Alex Ferguson's assistant at Manchester United.

SPAIN

Spain's arrival among the favourites to lift the World Cup in South Africa is based on their winning of the 2008 European Championship in style. The "Red Fury" want to be double champions.

Spain is finding favour with the bookmakers for the quick-moving game that saw them reach the 2010 World Cup finals as the only European team to win every one of their 10 qualifying group ties.

They began by thrashing Belgium 5-0 and confirmed their tickets to South Africa with a 3-0 win over Estonia.

In between they came from behind to win 2-1 in Belgium and Turkey, albeit by notching late winning goals in both games. Since Spain's new, and ultimately-successful, slick playing style was revealed to the world in 2008 opponents have tried, unsuccessfully, to stifle the game plan with a physical approach. Spain have continued to beat them with the technique and quick movement which saw them overcome World Cup holders Italy and Germany at Euro 2008 under coach Luis Aragones.

It is not unusual for an incoming coach to impose his own style on a team but Aragones' successor Vicente Del Bosque has adopted the adage "if it ain't broke don't fix it" and stuck with the "Aragones Plan".

He says: "Basically we've continued with what the squad have been doing."

There are always off days for successful sides and, ironically, Spain's came in South Africa at the Confederation's Cup of 2009. On a high from having just equalled Brazil's world record of 35 unbeaten games and having won their previous 15, the European champions suffered a shock 2-0 semi-final defeat to the United States and had to be content with third place in the tournament.

US manager Bob Bradley has made no secret of his game plan to target Spain's playmaker Xavi Hernandez and the midfield he commands. The idea was to never let the Spanish midfield settle into its usual controlling pattern.

Spanish captain and goalkeeper Iker Casillas admitted after the US game that his side had lost concentration – but not for long. Pride was restored when Spain battled back from 2-0 down to beat South Africa in extra time in the third-place match.

As Bradley correctly worked out, the key to

STAR PLAYER

FERNANDO TORRES
Born: March 20, 1984 • **Club:** Liverpool (England)

Torres is arguably the most complete striker ever to be produced by Spain and he proved it in front of millions when his right-foot chip settled the Euro 2008 final against Germany. It was not just the chip that impressed but the way he had the strength to hold off German full back Lahm, use his pace to run clear and the composure to finish with aplomb. Versatility is the key to Torres because he is used in different ways by club and country. As a lone striker for Liverpool he scores with both feet and his head but for Spain in harness with the mercurial David Villa the combination is one of the most potent in international soccer. Precocious Torres' first international with Spain was as a 19-year-old and he has gone on to win more than 70 caps.

ONES TO WATCH

XAVI HERNANDEZ
Born: January 25, 1980 • **Club:** Barcelona (Spain)

A World Cup medal from South Africa would give this compact midfielder an incredible treble – World, European and domestic champion all at the same time. Xavi, as he is known, is Spain's fulcrum, dropping deep to instigate moves, then driving forward to keep them flowing with telling passes. He was Euro 2008's "Player of the Tournament".

IKER CASILLAS
Born: May 20, 1981 • **Club:** Real Madrid (Spain)

The goalkeeper was another of Spain's current stars to have been blooded young in the international team. Like striker Torres he was just 19 after making his name as a teenager in Vicente Del Bosque's Real Madrid. Now regarded as one of the world's top goalkeepers, Spain's captain is closing in on Andoni Zubizareta's record of 126 Spanish caps and has already beaten his predecessor's tally of clean sheets for his country.

Spain's intricate game revolves around its midfield. Marcos Senna is the anchor while Barcelona's Xavi pulls the strings and Andres Iniesta puts together the probing passes and dribbles. Success in South Africa would give Xavi an amazing triple of success to go with his Euro 2008 and European Champions League 2009 medals.

Spain has an embarassment of midfield riches in that also in the squad are Real Madrid's Xabi Alonso or Arsenal's Cesc Fabregas who would feature in most international starting line-ups.

Tricky winger David Silva and strikers Fernando Torres and David Villa are together a very potent attacking threat and Villa is closing in on Raul's record of 44 goals for Spain.

Critics claim defence to be Spain's weak area, although Casillas is a world-class goalkeeper and the Spanish conceded only five goals in World Cup qualifying – and none against teams such as Italy, Russia and Germany in the knock-out stages of Euro 2008.

The quarter-final win over Italy in the European Championship was not only Spain's first competitive victory over the Italians but also showed they could withstand the pressure of a penalty shoot-out – and win. Euro 2008 success lifted a great weight from the shoulders of a country that had spawned great players and teams for decades but had not won a major championship since the Nations Cup in 1964.

With a World Cup best finish of fourth way back in 1950, Spain and the soccer-crazy Spanish people reckon its time has come to do well again by winning the World Cup.

MAN IN CHARGE

VICENTE DEL BOSQUE
Since taking the Spanish coaching role in 2008, Del Bosque has maintained continuity with his predecessor Luis Aragone's tactics and players. He is rated as one of the game's great man-managers in his own right and had to deal with huge egos as manager of the so-called "Galacticos" at Real Madrid. His players say his measured approach is an inspiration to them as it was when it spurred their quick recovery at last year's Confederation Cup after their defeat by the United States. Del Bosque was a victim of one of arguably the harshest of sackings when fired by Real Madrid in 2003. Having steered Real to Champions' League victories in 2000 and 2002, and Spanish titles in 2001 and 2003, he was dismissed a day after the 2003 league success because Madrid had lost in the European Cup semi-finals.

SWITZERLAND

The powers of recovery of Ottmar Hitzfeld's Switzerland squad cannot be underestimated in South Africa. The squad's stoical backs-to-the-wall attitude may be as useful in the World Cup Finals as they were in qualifying.

Switzerland overcame a terrible start to top Group Two of the European qualifiers to reach the finals as they had in 2006. Even coach Hitzfeld must have had momentarily doubts that Switzerland's chance was gone by the end of their second qualifier. Having let a 2-0 lead slip to draw with Israel, they crashed to an embarrassing 2-1 home defeat by Luxembourg. The enormity of this defeat, in which Fons Leweck netted the 87th-minute decider, was that this was tiny Luxembourg's first World Cup qualifying win in 36 years of trying.

It was now that Hitzfeld, known as "The General" for his strategic thinking, needed the experience with which he had steered German club sides Borussia Dortmund and Bayern Munich to Champions' League triumphs.

Reviving Switzerland's faltering 2010 World Cup campaign must rank as one of the most impressive achievements on his CV. Legendary German international goalkeeper Oliver Kahn, who worked with him at Bayern Munich, remembers that the coach's watchwords had always been "never to give up." Hitzfeld's philosophy was always "keep going", he said, and the coach put that into action during 2008-09 with Switzerland.

He remained calm, treated the draw and defeat as "blips" and concentrated on the future. He rightly described the next four games as "four cup finals" and his squad responded. Blaise N'Kufo's winner defeated Latvia 2-1and the process was repeated when the Swiss at last turned the group their way, with a 2-1 over Greece in Piraeus. Two more victories, both over Moldova, provided the momentum to beat Greece again, this time 2-0.

A draw in Latvia and a 3-0 revenge performance away to Luxembourg left Switzerland requiring only a point in their final game against Israel. The 0-0 home draw sufficed. Striker Eren Derdiyok described Hitzfeld as a "fantastic coach" with the organisational skills and calmness to get the best out of players – especially the younger ones.

Ironically Hitzfeld had rejected offers to coach his native Germany – and a much better chance of ultimate World Cup success – and opted for their

STAR PLAYER

ALEXANDER FREI
Born: July 15, 1979 • **Club:** FC Basel (Switzerland)

Time is running out for Swiss captain Frei to win a major international trophy. He needs to shine in South Africa as he will be 35 by the time Brazil 2014 comes around. But as Switzerland's all-time top scorer his country needs him in 2010 after he missed out on Euro 2008 with a knee ligament injury sustained in the opening game. He has won more than 70 caps and is the only Swiss player to rifle 40 international goals. He is also one of Switzerland's most successful soccer exports, scoring 48 goals in 100 games for Rennes and 31 in 69 appearances for Borussia Dortmund.

ONES TO WATCH

GOKHAN INLER
Born: June 27, 1984 • **Club:** Udinese (Italy)

Inler is the man from the land of clocks that makes his country's national team tick. Swiss-born but of Turkish descent, he is the energetic heart of the Swiss midfield where he plays deep industriously tackling and keeping a shrewd eye for a quick pass to keep play moving and the supply of chances to prolific strikers such as Frei.

PHILIPPE SENDEROS
Born: February 14, 1985 • **Club:** Arsenal (England)

Senderos' club and international careers are very different. The powerful defender has made himself a key figure for his country, although his club career in London has stuttered and stalled after a promising start. He has the physique and ability to be a dominant centre back and he is strong in the air at both ends of the pitch.

neighbour Switzerland with whom he had a long association.

As a player he turned out for Basel, Lugano and Luzern, before guiding Aarau to a Swiss Cup victory and Grasshoppers to two Swiss titles and two cup successes.

With flights booked to South Africa, Swiss expectations of their national team have already been realised. Fans regard reaching the finals as an achievement and if the team reached the last eight, Hitzfeld would, no doubt, become a national hero.

As a country with a small playing population to call upon, injuries and suspensions would hamper last-eight ambitions.

Switzerland have reached the last 16 twice in the past 16 years. In 1994, they lost 3-0 to Spain and in 2006 fell to a penalty shoot-out to Ukraine.

Swiss captain Alexander Frei is hoping to inspire his team to do better in South Africa. At 30, Switzerland's all-time international top scorer faces probably his last chance to shine in a major international tournament when he spearheads an attack which includes N'Kufo and Derdiyok.

Defensively, Switzerland's strengths lay with goalkeeper Diego Benaglio and the stability of veterans Grichting and Ludovic Magnin in the back line with centre-back Philippe Senderos. Switzerland has also been waiting

on the recovery of defender Johan Djourou after surgery on his left knee.

Tranquillo Barnetta and Gokhan Inler combine to run a neat and tidy midfield with the former supplementing the attack with occasional breaks forward and the latter enforcing a strong-tackling game. Pundits point to the Swiss lack of a goal-scoring midfielder unless Johan Vonlanthen can re-discover the form that saw him shine when only a teenager at Euro 2004.

MAN IN CHARGE

OTTMAR HITZFELD

Coaching Switzerland is probably Hitzfeld's last job. He says he is happy on the international scene and does not want, at 61, to move back to the hectic world of club management. Hitzfeld's CV shows him as one of the world's great coaches. He guided Borussia Dortmund to two Bundesliga titles and to a Champions' League triumph in 1997. Moving to Bayern Munich, he steered them to four Bundesliga championships and achieved victory in the 2001 Champions' League final after an unlucky defeat against Manchester United two years previously.

HONDURAS

Honduras can thank an American for their reaching the World Cup finals for only the second time in the country's history.

Honduras had done all they could to qualify for South Africa from the CONCACAF region with a 1-0 win in El Salvador but left the pitch believing they were out of the running for the third automatic place. The reason for their dejection was that 2,000 miles away in Washington DC, Costa Rica were leading group winners United States 2-1 – and were into stoppage time.

Honduras' saviour became US defender Jonathan Bornstein who headed an equaliser in the 4th minute of stoppage time to lift them into the third place which guaranteed qualification for the finals on goal difference. It also condemned the Costa Ricans to a play-off against Uruguay which they lost.

Honduras midfielder Julio De Leon recalled how "an almighty roar" from travelling supporters with radios alerted the team to the American goal. As the implications of getting to South Africa hit home he admits he dropped to the turf with emotion.

His coach Reinaldo Rueda was even later finding out as he had been banished from the bench during the El Salvador game after a row with the referee. He says after his sending off he went to the dressing room, got down on his knees and prayed for a miracle in the United States.

With three games left, the Hondurans had looked favourites to join the US and Mexico as automatic qualifiers but they lost two games on the trot – 1-0 to a late penalty in Mexico City and 3-2 at home to the US. Fortunately for Honduras, Costa Rica failed to take advantage and lost 1-0 to El Salvador. Striker Carlos Pavon was particularly grateful for the chance that El Salvador had given Honduras as he had failed to capitalise on several good scoring opportunities against the US.

The Honduran team became national heroes and their government declared a public holiday to mark the team's progress to the finals for the

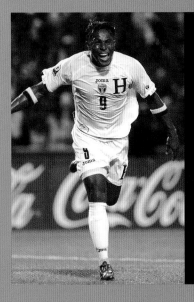

STAR PLAYER

CARLOS PAVON
Born: October 9, 1973 • **Club:** Real Espana (Spain)

Pavon is Honduras' all-time top scorer and a consistent match winner, netting more than 50 goals as he approaches 100 caps. He led the scorers in qualifying with seven goals, including the winner in El Salvador, and is the current Honduran Footballer of the Year. Pavon has travelled extensively in a chequered club career in which he has regularly topped scoring charts and is currently playing in Spain. He netted a famous hat-trick in Honduras's 3-1 win over Mexico in 2001. He says he is excited about going to South Africa after being through so many unsuccessful World Cup qualifying cycles over the years.

ONES TO WATCH

DAVID SUAZO

Born: November 5, 1979 • **Club:** Internazionale (Italy)

Suazo was once voted Italy's joint "Best Foreign Player" alongside AC Milan's Kaka and was the first Honduran to make an impact in Europe. After joining Cagliari in 1999 his form in Serie B earned him the nickname "The Panther". He helped Cagliari to promotion in 2004 and the 22 goals he scored in Serie A in 2006 and the 18 the following season brought him to the attention of Internazionale.

WILSON PALACIOS

Born: July 29, 1984 • **Club:** Tottenham Hotspur (England)

A dramatic change of role has made Palacios one of Honduras' most successful soccer exports. He began on the right of midfield for local team Olimpia and scored regularly. The vision of Wigan manager Steve Bruce, who took him to England, changed his career. Bruce thought Palacios' discipline, energy and tackling made him an ideal midfield anchor. Palacios agreed and has made the role his own – for Wigan, his new club Tottenham Hotspur and his country.

One of the major successes for coach Rueda has been the blending of the worldwise experience of his "foreign legion" with the best of the Honduran domestic league such as goalkeeper Noel Valladares, one of Central America's best, and left wing back Emilio Izaguirre.

In the eyes of Honduran soccer fans Rueda and his team have already achieved a great triumph by making the finals. The rest, as Pavon has been quoted as saying, is "icing on the cake."

first time since 1982. On that occasion they had been eliminated at the group stage.

The national hopes that they will go further this time in South Africa are based on the fact that Honduran stars now play all over the world. Among the main exports is forward David Suazo, who scored 95 league goals in 255 games in eight years with Italian club Cagliari, and who joined Jose Mourinho's Internazionale in a £9.5m deal and has had a loan spell with Portuguese giants Benfica.

De Leon has played for several top sides in Italy since 2001 and nippy right wing-back Edgar Alvarez is with Bari. Pavon's international soccer curriculum vitae includes Mexico, Spain and Italy – plus Los Angeles Galaxy in America's Major League Soccer (MLS).

Skipper Amado Guevara – the national team's engine – plays for Toronto in MLS while fellow midfielder Wilson Palacios has become an English Premiership star, with Wigan, then Tottenham. He became central America's most costly player when Spurs paid £15m for him in January 2009.

Full back Maynor Figueroa, is a Wigan regular and striker Carlos Costly – two-goal hero of the 4-0 home win over Costa Rica – plies his trade for Polish club GKS Belchatow.

MAN IN CHARGE

REINALDO RUEDA

The coach of Honduras is nicknamed "The Professor" for his patient and thoughtful approach and he has succeeded in giving his players a new confidence. Despite being Colombian-born he is a Honduran hero after guiding his adopted country to its first World Cup finals appearance for 28 years. He took over the Honduras squad in 2007 after coaching his homeland's national squad through the 2006 World Cup qualifiers but narrowly failed to get to the finals in Germany when they lost out to Uruguay for fifth place. He had previously steered Colombia's youngsters to victory in the 2000 Toulon Under-21 tournament and runners-up spot the following year.

CHILE

If unorthodox methods are the key to World Cup success then Chile might be in with a fighting chance in South Africa under Argentine-born coach Marcelo Bielsa.

Despite only having a brief and undistinguished playing career in his native Argentina which ended at 25, Bielsa has delivered Chile safely to the finals for the first time since 1998. He cut his international teeth with four years in charge of Argentina on the way to becoming one of South America's most-respected coaches – although his unconventional approach has earned him the nickname El Loco –Crazy One.

Argentina defender Roberto Ayala recalls Bielsa having strikers and midfielders training separately and at different times from the rest of the side. But he rates Bielsa as a soccer innovator and attributes him as one of the people from whom he learned most during his career.

Bielsa delivered his promised Chilean soccer revolution when a 4-2 qualifier win in Colombia saw them through to South Africa with a game to spare. Chile finished second in the South American group, a point behind the mighty Brazil and above his beloved Argentina who scraped in fourth.

Bielsa, whose brother Rafael and sister Maria Eugenia are senior politicians, saw his future in soccer leadership rather than politics. When he took over as Chile's national coach he says he set out to change the team's mentality and waxes lyrical about how good he feels when the team "spends more time attacking than defending." His positive approach is reflected in the successes in away qualifiers when they started their campaign with wins in Bolivia and Venezuela, before victories in Peru, Paraguay and Colombia clinched their finals' place.

With obvious mixed feelings Bielsa also guided Chile to their first-ever competitive victory over Argentina where the 1-0 win led to Argentine coach Alfio Basile quitting.

Qualifying was not a breeze for Bielsa. Chile were hit by injuries but overcame a 3-0 defeat at home to Paraguay to secure a string of vital away points. The coach brought back veteran striker Marcelo Salas who played his part in rallying fan and squad confidence.

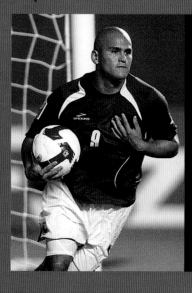

STAR PLAYER

HUMBERTO SUAZO
Born: May 10, 1981 • **Club:** Monterrey (Mexico)

Chile's ace poacher topped the qualifying scorers with 10 goals, including a stoppage-time winner in Venezuela. Suazo, who has netted more than 20 goals for Chile, is the latest in a line of prolific Chilean strikers such as Salas and Zamorano. He is relatively short but quick and strong in the box. He came to the big clubs' attention by scoring 40 goals in 40 games for third-division side San Luis in 2003–4. He continued to score freely for top-division club Audax, then averaged nearly a goal a game for Chilean giants Colo-Colo. Monterrey paid $8m to take him to Mexico in 2007 and has since become their top striker.

CLAUDIO BRAVO

Born: April 13, 1983 • **Club:** Real Sociedad (Spain)

Goalkeeper Bravo was an ever-present in Chile's qualifiers, playing every minute in the pressure cooker of 18 qualifiers. After making his international debut in 2004 he is now approaching 50 caps. He joined Real Sociedad in 2006 and has been a regular starter in Spain for the past two seasons. By current goalkeeping standards, he is not the biggest at 1.83m (6ft) but is a solid and reliable shot stopper.

ALEXIS SANCHEZ

Born: December 19, 1988 • **Club:** Udinese (Italy)

Sanchez has been a Chilean international since the age of 17 and, at 21, he remains Chile's bright, young hope. A tricky dribbler with an eye for goal, he has won more than 30 international caps. Udinese signed him for £2m in 2006, then loaned him to get experience at top Chilean club Colo-Colo and River Plate in Argentina. Sanchez has now established himself in Serie A.

Chile's potential was embodied in young players coming through. With the South Africa finals in mind, Bielsa has gone for youth by fast-tracking defender Arturo Vidal; midfielders Gary Medel, Mauricio Isla and Carlos Carmona; and striker Alexis Sanchez from the 2007 under-20 side which had finished third in their own World Cup.

In South Africa the spotlight will be on Bielsa's most lethal weapon, Humberto Suazo, who led the South America qualifying scorers with 10 goals. A late developer who admits to squandering his early soccer years, he will be 29 when he touches down in South Africa.

Chile will also be looking for more goals from Sanchez who has already carved himself a career in Italy with Udinese. His ability to weave past three or four defenders can make him a match winner and was sorely missed when he was one of those on the casualty list in the first four games of qualifying but he stormed back to score three vital goals. Sporting Lisbon's Matias Fernandez hit four from midfield.

Bielsa relies on goalkeeper and captain Claudio Bravo for on-field leadership, shrewd defensive organisation and a keen sense of responsibility. The keeper says that Bielsa has built an eager, hungry squad.

Support for the coach and his often-unconventional methods has also come from experienced midfielder Jorge Valdivia who says Bielsa has transformed everything from the state of the training camp to team discipline. He believes the way Chile is currently playing has earned them a new respect from opponents.

MAN IN CHARGE

MARCELO BIELSA

The World Cup finals are a familiar place for Bielsa. As Argentina coach from 1998 to 2004, he led his homeland to the 2002 finals. He cited insufficient energy for quitting Argentina and was out of the game for nearly three years before accepting the Chile job where he has energised his squad to the South Africa finals. Bielsa is searching still for the big prize as he had only modest success with Argentina, steering them to the final of the 2004 Copa America and to the Olympic soccer gold medal the same year. At club level he led Newell's Old Boys, for whom he once played, to the Copa Libertadores final in 1992 but lost to Brazil's Sao Paulo on penalties.

"Success is no accident. It is hard work, perseverance, learning, studying, sacrifice and most of all, love of what you are doing or learning to do." PELE

PLAYERS TO WATCH

STEVEN PIENAAR

Born: March 17, 1982
Club(s): Ajax Cape Town (1999–01), Ajax Amsterdam (Holland: 2001–06), Borussia Dortmund (Germany: 2006–08), Everton (Everton: loan 2007–08, permanent 2008–)
Position: Midfielder/winger

Playmaker Steven Pienaar has stepped off the substitutes' bench into the full glare of national expectation as his beloved South Africa hosts the 2010 World Cup finals – and he plans to shine.

The South Africa finals are a huge leap forward for Pienaar who, last time his country was at this stage in 2002, did not get a competitive kick. Fast forward eight years and expectations are high for his country's most-noted soccer export to be a major force in a good run in the tournament.

In 2002, Pienaar travelled with the squad to South Korea and Japan after having made his international debut only in the final warm-up match. He was left "warming" the substitutes' bench as South Africa was eliminated at the first-round stage.

Then the midfielder was only 20 and just establishing himself in Europe with Ajax in Holland after graduating from the Amsterdam club's nursery team, Ajax Cape Town. A move to the Dutch club led to five happy years and two league championship medals.

There was an unhappy interlude in Germany with Borussia Dortmund until Pienaar moved to England with Everton in 2008 for a bargain £2m transfer fee.

Pienaar's game is centred around insightful passing and darting runs and it has fitted in with the neat, well-drilled midfield at Everton where he has contributed to two consecutive fifth-place finishes in the English Premier League and a run to the 2009 FA Cup final. He was unfortunately on the losing side but became only the fifth South African to appear at the climax of the world's oldest cup competition.

Critics of Pienaar has said that he does not consistently reproduce his excellent club form in the colours of "Bafana Bafana" but he proved them wrong when South Africa had a few surprises up their sleeves to finish fourth in the 2009 Confederations Cup, also hosted by South Africa.

Pienaar had been dogged by an ankle injury in the run-up to the tournament before illness restricted him to only a late substitute appearance in the opening game, a 0-0 draw with Iraq.

South African fans got a close up of the maturity of Pienaar's game. He was influential in the displays that followed, including a 2-0 win over New Zealand and narrow, but confidence-building, losses to Brazil and Spain.

CRISTIANO RONALDO

Born: February 5, 1985
Club(s): Sporting Clube (2001–03),
Manchester United (England: 2003–09),
Real Madrid (Spain: 2009–)
Position: Forward

Love him or loathe him, Cristiano Ronaldo has it all going for him. The world's most expensive player at £80m is captain of a Portugal team which has a very realistic chance of becoming World Champions.

Ronaldo has more than the usual burdens to carry through the World Cup finals. He is the new captain of a country that has never quite achieved its full international potential. In South Africa he will come under close scrutiny as the leader of a potentially-new Portuguese "Golden Generation" and whether his performances are value for money in a world record transfer deal.

Ronaldo's transfer from England's Manchester United to Spain's Real Madrid did not just break all previous records; it smashed them by £14m.

There has been no doubt that 2008's "World Footballer of the Year", has been on an incredibly consistent goal-scoring streak for Manchester United. Every goal he scored in his six years in the English game was – ker-ching! – adding to the winger's value in United's cash register. During the club's Champions League-winning season of 2007–08, he scored 42 goals in all competitions. His final season with United had been described as a disappointment but he still scored 26 times and won another league title. Theoretically Ronaldo was a winger but Sir Alex Ferguson gave him plenty of latitude for a roaming role. He blasted powerful free kicks home with alacrity and penalties were his forte.

Yet he was ultimately good business for Manchester United who surprised the world in paying Lisbon's Sporting Clube £12m for the little-known teenager in 2003. The Madeira-born youngster set his play-acting, stepovers and arrogance before English fans who had not seen the like. United fans loved him; opposition fans gave him verbal Hell from the terraces.

Ronaldo is no lightweight mazy dribbler; his shooting is powerful, his heading forceful and his strength often made him unstoppable.

His flair was natural but Ronaldo's dedication to honing his physique and technique is enormous. Those explosive free kicks are the product of long hours on the training ground.

Even his vilification by England for his role in Wayne Rooney's red card at the 2006 World Cup did not faze him.

All of Portugal now looks to him for leadership, magic and goals to bring them to the peak of world soccer after the disappointments of being runners-up at Euro 2004 and fourth at the 2006 World Cup.

LIONEL MESSI

Born: June 24, 1987
Club(s): Barcelona (Spain: 2004–)
Position: Forward

Having been compared to the great Diego Maradona, Lionel Messi wants to emulate his illustrious predecessor in the Argentina No 10 shirt by winning the World Cup.

Despite his short stature Messi goes to South Africa with a massive reputation – and, officially, the world's best footballer. Since a couple of brief cameo appearances as his country disappointed with a quarter-final exit in Germany 2006, Messi's career has been one long upward curve culminating in an all-conquering 2008–09 season.

His 38 goals helped Barcelona to an unprecedented clean sweep of UEFA Champions League, Spanish league and cup titles. 1.69m (5ft 7in) Messi confounded the slights about his size and aerial ability when he scored the second of Barcelona's two goals in the Champions' League by outjumping England's 6ft 2in (1.89 m) centre back, Rio Ferdinand.

Now his task is to inspire Argentina in the South Africa finals after a near-disastrous qualifying campaign when for a long time the unthinkable seemed to be on the cards – a World Cup final tournament without Argentina and Messi.

Despite being born in Argentina, Messi has been at Barcelona since the age of 13 aided by the club's agreement to pay for growth hormone treatment.

What Barca have developed and invested in for a decade has come to fruition with Messi's prodigious dribbling skills and the ability to turn a game with a touch of genius. It has landed him with the "new Maradona" label – approved by Diego himself. The comparison suits Messi as he demonstrated with a recent goal for Barcelona against Getafe. His mazy solo run from the halfway line, was uncannily similar to Maradona's legendary second goal against England at the 1986 World Cup. And with shades of Maradona's infamous "Hand of God" goal against England, Messi has punched the ball into the net – and seen it stand.

Under Maradona's management of the national team Messi struggled initially to mirror his Barcelona form and scored only four goals in 18 games of a scrappy 2010 qualifying campaign.

Messi was much more influential as Argentina took Olympic gold at the Beijing Olympics and Argentina will be looking to him to replicate that to pick up another prestigious gold trophy in South Africa.

KAKA

Full name: Ricardo Izecson dos Santos Leite
Born: April 22, 1982
Club(s): Sao Paulo (2001–03), AC Milan
(Italy: 2003–09), Real Madrid (Spain: 2009–)
Position: Forward

This time around Kaka wants to be involved all the way if Brazil are to win the World Cup a sixth time in South Africa. Much has happened for the star since his brief 25 minutes of fame eight years ago.

Although he has already experienced the joy of being in the World Cup-winning squad of 2002, Kaka was not the finished article. Since playing those few minutes against Costa Rica in the first round, his vision, poise on the ball and prolific strike-rate have made him a global icon.

Kaka has achieved a great deal, including briefly being the world's costliest player but he still hankers for a World Cup win in which he is fully involved.

He clinched the "World Footballer of the Year" award in 2007 after setting up both AC Milan's goals in their UEFA Champions League Final win over Liverpool.

The previous year had been frustrating for Kaka as one of Brazil's most effective players in a vain defence of their world cup crown. With such a talent-packed team, Kaka was cramped for space in between Ronaldinho and Ronaldo as Brazil failed to gel and fell to France in the quarter-finals.

Pious and self-effacing, Kaka's response, for both club and country, was calmly to put in the performances for which AC Milan had spent £5.5m to bring him from Sao Paulo in 2003.

Milan supporters loved him and Kaka staged outraged protests when the club came close to selling him to Manchester City for a price quoted at an astronomical £100m-plus.

However, it was Real Madrid who got Kaka in 2009 when they paid Milan a then world record of £55m. Kaka was part of the Spanish club's new "Galacticos" project and were later to break the world record again by pairing him with £80m Cristiano Ronaldo.

It was business as usual on the pitch for Kaka as he inspired his country to success at the 2009 FIFA Confederations Cup in South Africa. He was named man of the match after Brazil's thrilling comeback in the final against the United States,

then picked up the Golden Ball as player of the tournament.

But from lying partially paralysed as an 18-year-old after fracturing his spine in a fall from a diving board, for Kaka to blossom into one of the finest players of his era would have seemed impossible.

With such life experiences and an undoubted world-class football talent, few would bet against Kaka inspiring Brazil to another World Cup triumph in South Africa this summer.

MICHAEL BALLACK

Born: September 26, 1976
Club(s): Chemnitzer FC (1995–1997),
1. FC Kaiserslautern (1997–1999), Bayer
Leverkusen (1999–2002), Bayern Munich
(2002–2006), Chelsea (England: 2006–)
Position: Midfielder

Germany's Michael Ballack is running out of time in his quest for a major prize. At 33 he is hoping to drive his country to a World Cup win that he has been part of.

Ballack wants to shake off being a "nearly man" in major competitions. He was a runner up at the 2002 World Cup and 2008 European Championships; third in 2006's World Cup; and has twice come second in the European Champions' League.

His mission with Germany is to atone for that catalogue of near misses and he can do it because, as the captain, he is a driving force and inspiration to his team-mates.

He showed this in getting Germany to the 2002 World Cup final against Brazil but missed the defeat by Brazil through suspension. It capped a particularly miserable 2001–02 season for Ballack, who finished a four-time runner up – in the World Cup and, with his club Bayer Leverkusen, the UEFA Champions League, Bundesliga and German Cup.

However, he was later to have more successful league and cup-winning spells at Bayern Munich and current club Chelsea.

Ballack is undoubtedly the outstanding German soccer of his generation for his inspiration, work rate and pin-sharp passing. Deeper-lying roles for both club and country have made him no less a threat for a powerful strike at goal.

While the major international trophies have eluded Ballack, his club successes are a thick catalogue. His first season with Kaiserslautern brought a Bundesliga title in 1997–98 and his move to Bayern Munich in 2002 was followed by two league and cup doubles. His first task after being appointed the national team captain was to lead Germany as the host nation to third place in the 2006 World Cup.

Ballack became the highest paid footballer in England, after an end-of-contract free transfer to Chelsea but his time at Stamford Bridge has been troubled by injuries and media comments about his commitment.

The fateful number 2 jinx hit him again with Chelsea when he lost out to Manchester United for several Premiership titles and in an all-English Champions' League Final.

Ballack always battles back and if anyone can inspire Germany to greater heights in 2010, he can.

GIANLUIGI BUFFON

Born: January 28, 1978
Club(s): Parma (1995–2001),
Juventus (2001–)
Position: Goalkeeper

Italy's bid for a second consecutive World Cup win rests very much on their "Tower of Strength" goalkeeper Gianluigi Buffon. With his commanding presence, Italy could emulate their two-in-a-row successes of 1934 and 1938.

Buffon's agility and charismatic penalty-box presence was a huge influence on Italy's successful run to the world championship in 2006 and reliance on that again in South Africa could inspire the present crop of Italian stars to equal Brazil's record of five World Cup wins.

As Italy's team left the corruption scandal raging at home behind them to lift a fourth World Cup, Buffon conceded only two goals during the whole tournament. One was an own goal by a defender; the other a Zinedine Zidane penalty in the final against France.

Buffon commands not only his penalty area but also respect and inspires assurance among his defenders. Many a striker has felt a flash of fear to see the big 1.91 m (6ft 3in) frame of Buffon advancing on them from his goal.

He remains the world's most expensive goalkeeper. He was sold from Parma to Juventus for £30m a decade ago and one can only speculate on what his cost would be at 2010 prices. Certainly Italy fans are convinced he was worth every penny.

And so is his club Juventus who have been repaid with not only title-winning performances but also loyalty. When the mighty Juventus were punished for corruption offences by being relegated to Italy's Serie B, many of their top players headed for the door. Buffon stayed and helped the club bounce back into the top division.

A Buffon as a goalkeeper on the Italy teamsheet is a case of déjà vu as Lorenzo, a distant cousin of Gianluigi, won 16 Italian caps in the late 1950s-early 1960s.

Gianluigi had a sporting heritage with his father a weightlifter and his mother a discus thrower. After being a member of Italy's triumphant team at the Under-21 European Championship, he made his full Italy debut at 17 in 1997. At club level

Parma lifted the treble of UEFA Cup, Italian Cup and Italian Supercup in 1999.

With Juventus he had four Serie A title triumphs, even though two were later rescinded in the corruption scandal. For club or country, reliable handling, bravery and presence have been his trademarks and knowing that Buffon is behind them is enough to give the Italians confidence about taking another World Cup in 2010.

WAYNE ROONEY

Born: October 24, 1985
Club(s): Everton (2002–2004),
Manchester United (2004–)
Position: Forward

Wayne Rooney is the talisman for England's hopes of finally winning a second World Cup. His goal-scoring abilities are flawless – his temperament less so.

Things can get dramatic with the Manchester United striker around. He remains his country's youngest goal scorer thanks to a neat finish against Macedonia in 2003 but twice the fates have conspired to destroy his hopes of a major tournament victory.

He made the headlines at the 2004 European Championship with four goals against Switzerland and Croatia which were struck with maturity and panache. Then a broken foot bone saw him limp out early fromEngland's quarter-final defeat to Portugal.

He was removed early from England's 2006 World Cup bid when Portugal were again quarter-final opponents. But this time he was sent off in disgrace for stamping on centre-back Ricardo Carvalho with the petulance explained by his frustration at a lack of fitness after rushing back from a pre-finals foot injury.

But England fans love Rooney for his battling spirit and his skilful feet and he first shot to fame aged 16 with a spectacular last-minute Premier League winner for his club Everton. A year later he became, at the time, England's youngest international.

The reputation for a fiery temper did not stop Manchester United manager Sir Alex Ferguson paying £25.6m to sign him from Everton in 2004. This was a cue for another Rooney dramatic entrance – scoring a European Champions' League hat-trick against Fenerbahce on his United debut.

Since moving to Old Trafford, he has won the Champions' League, several Premier League titles, the Carling Cup and the World Club Cup at which he scored the winning goal.

Rooney has conceded that he should score more goals but Ferguson prefers to harness his tireless work-rate on the wings instead of granting the player's wish to be a centre forward.

England coach Fabio Capello seems to have brought out the prolific best in Rooney. Across the European qualifying groups for the 2010 World Cup only Greece's Theofanis Gekas scored more than Rooney's nine in nine matches.

England fans believe that Rooney is so crucial to their cause that they might have reached the 2008 European Championship finals had an ankle injury not ruled Rooney out of a decisive qualifier against Croatia.

South Africa is an opportunity to keep his head and make up for lost time for England.

FERNANDO TORRES

Born: March 20, 1984
Club(s): Atletico de Madrid (2001–2007), Liverpool (England: 2007–)
Position: Centre-forward

If favourites Spain are to win the World Cup in 2010 Fernando Torres is tipped as the man to help them do it. Their star striker is a big-occasion player capable of the important goals at just the right time.

He has a pedigree for vital goals and he demonstrated it with the deft winner against Germany in the final of the 2008 European Championship to end his country's 44-year wait for a trophy.

At an even younger age he had performed similar feats – against France in the Under-16 European Championship Final in 2001 and again versus Germany in the Under-19 European Championship the following year.

As one of the most promising young talents in Europe, Torres was 17 when he made his league debut for boyhood favourites Atletico de Madrid in 2001. Atletico fans adored him, both for his control, pace and prolific goal-scoring and his loyalty in a city dominated by Real Madrid.

Nineteen was a fantastic age for Torres, whose nickname was "El Niño" (The Kid). He was made club captain and got his international call up. He celebrated with three goals during Spain's four matches at the 2006 World Cup finals. Eventually, after fending off many bids for Torres, Atletico could not resist Liverpool's huge £25m bid

Typically Torres proved an instant hit in the English Premier League and his 24 league goals in 2007–08 – including two hat-tricks – were the best first-season haul of any foreign arrival in England's top division.

Better was to come with Torres's Euro 2008-winning exploits. He and strike partner David Villa were named in the official team of the tournament and Torres later finished third in the 2008 World Footballer of the Year rankings.

With Spain the bookmakers favourites, Torres, as part of one of the most talented Spanish squads for decades, will be looking to forward to a strong World Cup and will be a clear contender to become the tournament's top scorer.

The last time Torres was in South Africa, he scored the fastest international hat-trick in Spain's history – taking just 17 minutes to put three past New Zealand in the first round of the 2009 Confederations Cup.

As a player who can repeat great exploits, Spanish fans will be hoping South Africa will inspire Torres again.

"Beauty comes first. Victory is secondary. What matters is joy."
SOCRATES

WORLD CUP HISTORY

WORLD CUP HISTORY

The World Cup is soccer's most prestigious tournament. First contested by just 13 countries in 1930 more countries now enter the World Cup than there are members of the United Nations. But it wasn't always that way...

As interest in soccer spread around the world, a global governing body was required to regulate it and, in Paris in 1904, the Federation Internationale de Football was set up. Frenchman Robert Guérin, the guiding light, was named FIFA's first president. Guérin was succeeded as President by compatriot Jules Rimet and, at a special FIFA Congress in Amsterdam, he agreed to clamour for a world professional championship by organising the first World Cup, to be staged in 1930 – midway between the Olympic Games tournaments.

Uruguay were the first hosts and winners, but the inaugural tournament wasn't quite the meticulously run competition it is today. A trainer knocked himself unconscious when he inhaled from a broken bottle of chloroform he was bringing onto the pitch to treat an injured player. France's game with Argentina ended six minutes early and only resumed after a near riot.

Uruguay and Argentina couldn't agree on a match-ball for the Final, so each provided them for one half.

Tournament founder Jules Rimet presents the first World Cup trophy to Uruguayan soccer officials following the South American team's 4-2 win in the Final.

URUGUAY 1930

The cost of travelling to South America was too steep for most European countries, despite the hosts and defending Olympic champions, Uruguay, offering to pay the travel costs. Uruguay had been chosen as hosts not only because of that offer but they wanted to celebrate the country's centenary in style and they would build new stadiums too. Thus, the inaugural World Cup comprised 13 nations, with Belgium, France, Romania and Yugoslavia all sailing on the same liner. Lucien Laurent scored the first ever World Cup goal in France's 4–1 opening defeat of Mexico. In the semi-finals, Argentina faced the United States and Uruguay met Yugoslavia. The two South Americans were too strong, both winning 6–1, to set up the Final in Montevideo. Although Pablo Dorado gave Uruguay an early lead, Carlos Peucelle and Guillermo Stabile made it 2–1 to Argentina at half-time. Uruguay dominated the second half and goals from Pedro Cea, Victoriano Iriarte and Hector Castro gave them a 4–2 victory and they became the first World Cup winners.

POOL 1

France	4	Mexico	1
Argentina	1	France	0
Chile	3	Mexico	0
Chile	1	France	0
Argentina	6	Mexico	3
Argentina	3	Chile	1

	P	W	D	L	F	A	Pts
Argentina	3	3	0	0	10	4	6
Chile	3	2	0	1	5	3	4
France	3	1	0	2	4	3	2
Mexico	3	0	0	3	4	13	0

POOL 2

Yugoslavia	2	Brazil	1
Yugoslavia	4	Bolivia	0
Brazil	4	Bolivia	0

	P	W	D	L	F	A	Pts
Yugoslavia	2	2	0	0	6	1	4
Brazil	2	1	0	1	5	2	2
Bolivia	2	0	0	2	0	8	0

POOL 3

Romania	3	Peru	1
Uruguay	1	Peru	0
Uruguay	4	Romania	0

	P	W	D	L	F	A	Pts
Uruguay	2	2	0	0	5	0	4
Romania	2	1	0	1	3	5	2
Peru	2	0	0	2	1	4	0

POOL 4

USA	3	Belgium	0
USA	3	Paraguay	0
Paraguay	1	Belgium	0

	P	W	D	L	F	A	Pts
USA	2	2	0	0	6	0	4
Paraguay	2	1	0	1	1	3	2
Belgium	2	0	0	2	0	4	0

SEMI-FINALS

Argentina	6	USA	1
Uruguay	6	Yugoslavia	1

FINAL – July 30: Centenario, Montevideo

Uruguay 4 (Dorado 12, Cea 57, Iriarte 68, Castro 90)
Argentina 2 (Peucelle 20, Stabile 37)
HT: 1–2. **Att:** 93,000. **Ref:** Langenus (Belgium)
Uruguay: Ballestreros, Nasazzi, Mascheroni, Andrade, Fernandez, Gestido, Dorado, Scarone, Castro, Cea, Iriarte. **Argentina:** Botasso, Della Torre, Paternoster, Evaristo, Monti, Suarez, Peucelle, Varallo, Stabile, Ferreira, Evaristo.
Top scorer: 8 Stabile (Argentina)

ITALY 1934

Uruguay refused to defend their championship in Italy in 1934, in protest at so many European countries failing to travel to their country four years earlier. The hosts, coached by Vittorio Pozzo, were under huge pressure from the dictator Benito Mussolini to prove that his way was the best, and they eventually delivered. With 16 countries qualifying for the finals, the tournament was played on a straight knock-out and all eight quarter-finalists were from Europe. Austria's Wunderteam, led by Andreas Sindelaar, reached the semi-finals with a victory over Hungary, but Italy, who recorded the first clean sheet of the finals in a quarter-final replay against Spain, beat them 1–0 to reach the Final. Czechoslovakia were the other finalists, having beaten Romania, Switzerland and Germany on the way. The Final went to extra time after Raimondo Orsi, a losing finalist with Argentina four years earlier, cancelled out Antonin Puc's opener, both goals coming in the last 15 minutes. Five minutes into extra time, Angelo Schiavio scored what proved to be the winner.

FIRST ROUND

Italy	7	USA	1
Czechoslovakia	2	Romania	1
Germany	5	Belgium	2
Austria	3	France	2*
Spain	3	Brazil	1
Switzerland	3	Holland	2
Sweden	3	Argentina	2
Hungary	4	Egypt	2

* After extra time

SECOND ROUND

Germany	2	Sweden	1
Austria	2	Hungary	1
Italy	1	Spain	1*
Italy	1	Spain	0r
Czechoslovakia	3	Switzerland	2

* After extra time; r=Replay

SEMI-FINALS

Czechoslovakia	3	Germany	1
Italy	1	Austria	0

THIRD-PLACE MATCH

Germany	3	Austria	2

FINAL – June 10: Flaminio, Rome

*Italy 2 (Orsi 81, Schiavio 95)
Czechoslovakia 1 (Puc 71)
HT: 0-0. 90min: 1-1. **Att:** 55,000. **Ref:** Eklind (Sweden)
Italy: Combi, Monzeglio, Allemandi, Ferraris IV, Monti, Bertolini, Guaita, Meazza, Schiavio, Ferrari, Orsi.
Czechoslovakia: Planicka, Zenisek, Ctyroky, Kostalek, Cambal, Kreil, Junek, Svoboda, Sobotka, Nejedly, Puc.
Top scorers: 5 Nejedly (Czechoslovakia), Schiavio (Italy), Conen (Germany).

* After extra time

FRANCE 1938

Europe again hosted the 1938 finals, prompting Argentina and Uruguay, once more, to boycott the event. Hosts France beat Belgium 3–1, but lost by the same score to Italy in the quarter-final. Two countries made what would be their only finals appearance: Cuba and the Dutch East Indies (now Indonesia), the former beating Romania in a replay before losing 8–0 to Sweden, the latter going down 6–0 to Hungary in the first round. The most extraordinary match of the finals was Brazil's first round 6–5 extra-time victory against Poland. Both teams' centre-forwards, Leonidas and Ernst Willimowski, scored hat-tricks. Brazil made it to the semi-finals, where defending champions Italy triumphed 2–1. Hungary were the other finalists, beating Sweden 5–1 in the last four. A much-changed Italian team, coach Pozzo kept only Giuseppe Meazza and Giaonin Ferrari from the 1934 winning eleven, were too strong for the Hungarians, with Gino Colaussi and Silvio Piola both netting twice in a 4–2 victory. Pal Titkos and Gyorgy Sarosi scored for Hungary.

FIRST ROUND

Switzerland	1	Germany	1*
Switzerland	4	Germany	2r
Cuba	3	Romania	3*
Cuba	2	Romania	1r
Hungary	6	Dutch East Indies	0
France	3	Belgium	1
Czechoslovakia	3	Holland	0*
Brazil	6	Poland	5*
Italy	2	Norway	1*

* After extra time; r=Replay

SECOND ROUND

Sweden	8	Cuba	0
Hungary	2	Switzerland	0
Italy	3	France	1
Brazil	1	Czechoslovakia	1*
Brazil	2	Czechoslovakia	1r

* After extra time; r=Replay

SEMI-FINALS

Italy	2	Brazil	1
Hungary	5	Sweden	1

THIRD-PLACE MATCH

Brazil	4	Sweden	2

FINAL – June 19: Colombes, Paris

Italy 4 (Colaussi 5, 35, Piola 16, 82)
Hungary 2 (Titkos 7, Sarosi 70)
HT: 3-1. **Att:** 55,000. **Ref:** Capdeville (France).
Italy: Olivieri, Foni, Andreolo, Rava, Serantoni, Locatelli, Biavati, Meazza, Piola, Ferrari, Colaussi.
Hungary: Szabo, Polgar, Biro, Szalay, Szucs, Lazar, Sas, Vincze, Sarosi, Szengeller, Titkos.
Top scorer: 7 Leonidas (Brazil); 7 Szengeller (Hungary); 5 Piola (Italy).

BRAZIL 1950

The first post-World War 2 World Cup was staged in Brazil and the first round witnessed one of the greatest to date and still one of the most stunning results in international soccer: USA 1, England 0. England failed to reach the final group – there were no knock-out rounds – as did Italy, but the Azzurri were still recovering from the Superga plane disaster which killed the Torino team, including ten internationals. The final group stage comprised Brazil, Spain, Sweden and Uruguay and, by happy coincidence the last of the group matches was effectively the World Cup final, with Brazil needing a draw and Uruguay a win to become world champions. Close to 200,000 fanatical Brazilians at the Maracana Stadium in Rio de Janeiro watched Friaca score two minutes into the second half. Juan Schiaffino equalised for Uruguay midway through the second half and then, with 11 minutes to go, the unthinkable happened to Brazil: Alcides Ghiggia scored what proved to be the winner for Uruguay. The Celestes now had the amazing record of winning the World Cup every time they entered.

POOL 1

Brazil	4	Mexico	0
Yugoslavia	3	Switzerland	0
Yugoslavia	4	Mexico	1
Brazil	2	Switzerland	2
Brazil	2	Yugoslavia	0
Switzerland	2	Mexico	1

	P	W	D	L	F	A	Pts
Brazil	3	2	1	0	8	2	5
Yugoslavia	3	2	0	1	7	3	4
Switzerland	3	1	1	1	4	6	3
Mexico	3	0	0	3	2	10	0

POOL 2

Spain	3	USA	1
England	2	Chile	0
USA	1	England	0
Spain	2	Chile	0
Spain	1	England	0
Chile	5	USA	2

	P	W	D	L	F	A	Pts
Spain	3	3	0	0	6	1	6
England	3	1	0	2	2	2	2
Chile	3	1	0	2	5	6	2
USA	3	1	0	2	4	8	2

POOL 3

Sweden	3	Italy	2
Sweden	2	Paraguay	2
Italy	2	Paraguay	0

	P	W	D	L	F	A	Pts
Sweden	2	1	1	0	5	4	3
Italy	2	1	0	1	4	3	2
Paraguay	2	0	1	1	2	4	1

POOL 4

Uruguay	8	Bolivia	0

	P	W	D	L	F	A	Pts
Uruguay	1	1	0	0	8	0	2
Bolivia	1	0	0	1	0	8	0

FINAL POOL

Uruguay	2	Spain	2
Brazil	7	Sweden	1
Uruguay	3	Sweden	2
Brazil	6	Spain	1
Sweden	3	Spain	1
Uruguay	2	Brazil	1

	P	W	D	L	F	A	Pts
Uruguay	3	2	1	0	7	5	5
Brazil	3	2	0	1	14	4	4
Sweden	3	1	0	2	6	11	2
Spain	3	0	1	2	4	11	1

FINAL – July 16: Maracana, Rio de Janeiro

Brazil 1 (Friaca 47)
Uruguay 2 (Schiaffino 66, Ghiggia 79)
HT: 0-0. **Att:** 199,854. **Ref:** Reader (England)
Brazil: Barbosa, Da Costa, Juvenal, Bauer, Alvim, Bigode, Friaca, Zizinho, Ademir, Jair, Chico.
Uruguay: Maspoli, Gonzales, Tejera, Gambetta, Varela, Andrade, Ghiggia, Perez, Miguez, Schiaffino, Moran.
Top scorer: Top scorer: 7 Ademir (Brazil)

SWITZERLAND 1954

FIFA celebrated its golden jubilee by awarding the 1954 World Cup to its home country, Switzerland. Hungary, on a four-year unbeaten streak, were hot favourites to win the competition. It was a goal-crazy tournament. Five Group 2 matches produced 41 goals, Hungary routing South Korea 9–0 and West Germany 8–3 (the Koreans also lost 7–0 to Turkey, who later lost a play-off match 7–2 to the Germans), and a record 12 goals came in a quarter-final between Austria and Switzerland, the former triumphing 7–5 despite a hat-trick from Sepp Huegi. An ankle injury inflicted on Hungary's Ferenc Puskas by German defender Werner Liebrich meant he missed 4–2 victories over Brazil and Uruguay – their first ever World Cup defeat – but he was recalled for their second meeting in the Final. Puskas and Zoltan Czibor gave Hungary a quickfire 2–0 lead, but Max Morlock and Helmut Rahn soon tied it up. Rahn scored again six minutes from time to end Hungary's unbeaten run and give West Germany the World Cup.

POOL 1

Yugoslavia	1	France	0
Brazil	5	Mexico	0
France	3	Mexico	2
Brazil	1	Yugoslavia	1

	P	W	D	L	F	A	Pts
Brazil	2	1	1	0	6	1	3
Yugoslavia	2	1	1	0	2	1	3
France	2	1	0	1	3	3	2
Mexico	2	0	0	2	2	8	0

POOL 2

Hungary	9	South Korea	0
West Germany	4	Turkey	1
Hungary	8	West Germany	3
Turkey	7	South Korea	0

	P	W	D	L	F	A	Pts
Hungary	2	2	0	0	17	3	4
West Germany	2	1	0	1	7	9	2
Turkey	2	1	0	1	8	4	2
South Korea	2	0	0	2	0	16	0

POOL 3

Austria	1	Scotland	0
Uruguay	2	Czechoslovakia	0
Austria	5	Czechoslovakia	0
Uruguay	7	Scotland	0

	P	W	D	L	F	A	Pts
Uruguay	2	2	0	0	9	0	4
Austria	2	2	0	0	6	0	4
Czechoslovakia	2	0	0	2	0	7	0
Scotland	2	0	0	2	0	8	0

POOL 4

England	4	Belgium	4
England	2	Switzerland	0
Switzerland	2	Italy	1
Italy	4	Belgium	1

	P	W	D	L	F	A	Pts
England	2	1	1	0	6	4	3
Italy	2	1	0	1	5	3	2
Switzerland	2	1	0	1	2	3	2
Belgium	2	0	1	1	5	8	1

PLAY-OFF
| Switzerland | 4 | Italy | 1 |
| West Germany | 7 | Turkey | 2 |

QUARTER-FINALS
West Germany	2	Yugoslavia	0
Hungary	4	Brazil	2
Austria	7	Switzerland	5
Uruguay	4	England	2

SEMI-FINALS
| West Germany | 6 | Austria | 1 |
| Hungary | 4 | Uruguay | 2 |

THIRD-PLACE MATCH
| Austria | 3 | Uruguay | 1 |

FINAL – July 4: Wankdorf, Bern
West Germany 3 (Morlock 10, Rahn 18, 82)
Hungary 2 (Puskas 6, Czibor 8)
HT: 2-2. **Att:** 60,000. **Ref:** Ling (England)
West Germany: Turek, Posipal, Liebrich, Kohlmeyer, Eckel, Mai, Rahn, Morlock, O Walter, F Walter, Schafer.
Hungary: Grosics, Buzansky, Lorant, Lantos, Bozsik, Zakarias, Czibor, Kocsis, Hidegkuti, Puskas, Toth.
Top scorer: 11 Kocsis (Hungary)

SWEDEN 1958

Eight years after missing out on home soil, Brazil travelled to Sweden and became the first nation to win the World Cup outside of their own continent. Having ditched their "unlucky" white kit for a yellow/blue/green one to match their flag, the introduction of Didi, Vava, Garrincha and, most notably, 17-year-old Pele was even more eye-catching. All four British teams qualified for the finals, and England and Wales both fell to Brazil, the latter, in the quarter-final, being the first team to concede a goal to Pele. As great as Brazil were, the man of the tournament was French striker Just Fontaine, who scored a single-tournament record 13 goals in six matches. Sweden battled all the way to the Final, where they ran into a rampant Brazil team, which replied to Nils Liedholm's fourth-minute goal with two from Vava before half-time, and two from Pele (his fifth and six of the finals) and one from Garrincha after the break on their way to a 5–2 victory.

POOL 1
West Germany	3	Argentina	1
Northern Ireland	1	Czechoslovakia	0
West Germany	2	Czechoslovakia	2
Argentina	3	Northern Ireland	1
West Germany	2	Northern Ireland	2
Czechoslovakia	6	Argentina	1

	P	W	D	L	F	A	Pts
West Germany	3	1	2	0	7	5	4
Czechoslovakia	3	1	1	1	8	4	3
N. Ireland	3	1	1	1	4	5	3
Argentina	3	1	0	2	5	10	2

POOL 2

France	7	Paraguay	3
Yugoslavia	1	Scotland	1
Yugoslavia	3	France	2
Paraguay	3	Scotland	2
France	2	Scotland	1
Yugoslavia	3	Paraguay	3

	P	W	D	L	F	A	Pts
France	3	2	0	1	11	7	4
Yugoslavia	3	1	2	0	7	6	4
Paraguay	3	1	1	1	9	12	3
Scotland	3	0	1	2	4	6	1

POOL 3

Sweden	3	Mexico	0
Hungary	1	Wales	1
Wales	1	Mexico	1
Sweden	2	Hungary	1
Sweden	0	Wales	0
Hungary	4	Mexico	0

	P	W	D	L	F	A	Pts
Sweden	3	2	1	0	5	1	5
Hungary	3	1	1	1	6	3	3
Wales	3	0	3	0	2	2	3
Mexico	3	0	1	2	1	8	1

POOL 4

England	2	Soviet Union	2
Brazil	3	Austria	0
England	0	Brazil	0
Soviet Union	2	Austria	0
Brazil	2	Soviet Union	0
England	2	Austria	2

	P	W	D	L	F	A	Pts
Brazil	3	2	1	0	5	0	5
England	3	0	3	0	4	4	3
Soviet Union	3	1	1	1	4	4	3
Austria	3	0	1	2	2	7	1

PLAY-OFF
Northern Ireland	2	Czechoslovakia	1
Wales	2	Hungary	1
Soviet Union	1	England	0

QUARTER-FINALS
France	4	Northern Ireland	0
West Germany	1	Yugoslavia	0
Sweden	2	Soviet Union	0
Brazil	1	Wales	0

SEMI-FINALS
| Brazil | 5 | France | 2 |
| Sweden | 3 | West Germany | 1 |

THIRD-PLACE MATCH
| France | 6 | West Germany | 3 |

FINAL – June 29: Rasunda, Stockholm
Brazil 5 (Vava 9, 30, Pele 55, 90, Zagalo 68)
Sweden 2 (Liedholm 4, Simonsson 80)
HT: 2-1. **Att:** 49,737. **Ref:** Guigue (France)
Brazil: Gilmar, D Santos, Bellini, Orlando, N Santos, Zito, Didi, Garrincha, Vava, Pele, Zagalo.
Sweden: Svensson, Bergmark, Gustavsson, Axbom, Borjesson, Parling, Hamrin, Gren, Simonsson, Liedholm, Skoglund.
Top scorer: 13 Fontaine (France)

CHILE 1962

Brazil became the second nation to retain the World Cup and they did so despite losing Pele for the knock-out rounds. The Seleçao reacted by going from their 4-2-4 formation of 1958 to 4-3-3 in Chile, using Garrincha as a centre-forward. He scored twice to knock out England in the quarter-final, and twice in the semi-final against Chile – before being sent off (he was cleared to play in the Final). The most memorable match of the finals was "the battle of Santiago", which saw two Italians dismissed by English referee Ken Aston, who missed Chile's Leonel Sanchez breaking Humberto Maschio's nose with a vicious punch. Brazil may not have been as

entertaining as four years earlier, but they were equally successful, defeating Czechoslovakia 3-1 in the Final. Again they fell behind, European Footballer of the Year-in-waiting Josef Masopust scoring after 15 minutes. Amarildo soon equalised and second half goals from Zito and Vava sealed Brazil's second successive World Cup title.

GROUP 1

Uruguay	2	Colombia	1
Soviet Union	2	Yugoslavia	0
Yugoslavia	3	Uruguay	1
Soviet Union	4	Colombia	4
Soviet Union	2	Uruguay	1
Yugoslavia	5	Colombia	0

	P	W	D	L	F	A	Pts
Soviet Union	3	2	1	0	8	5	5
Yugoslavia	3	2	0	1	8	3	4
Uruguay	3	1	0	2	4	6	2
Colombia	3	0	1	2	5	11	1

GROUP 2

Chile	3	Switzerland	1
West Germany	0	Italy	0
Chile	2	Italy	0
West Germany	2	Switzerland	1
Italy	3	Switzerland	0
West Germany	2	Chile	0

	P	W	D	L	F	A	Pts
West Germany	3	2	1	0	4	1	5
Chile	3	2	0	1	5	3	4
Italy	3	1	1	1	3	2	3
Switzerland	3	0	0	3	2	8	0

GROUP 3

Brazil	2	Mexico	0
Czechoslovakia	1	Spain	0
Brazil	0	Czechoslovakia	0
Spain	1	Mexico	0
Brazil	2	Spain	1
Mexico	3	Czechoslovakia	1

	P	W	D	L	F	A	Pts
Brazil	3	2	1	0	4	1	5
Czechoslovakia	3	1	1	1	2	3	3
Mexico	3	1	0	2	3	4	2
Spain	3	1	0	2	2	3	2

GROUP 4

Argentina	1	Bulgaria	0
Hungary	2	England	1
England	3	Argentina	1
Hungary	6	Bulgaria	1
Argentina	0	Hungary	0
England	0	Bulgaria	0

	P	W	D	L	F	A	Pts
Hungary	3	2	1	0	8	2	5
England	3	1	1	1	4	3	3
Argentina	3	1	1	1	2	3	3
Bulgaria	3	0	1	2	1	7	1

QUARTER-FINALS
Yugoslavia	1	West Germany	0
Brazil	3	England	1
Chile	2	Soviet Union	1
Czechoslovakia	1	Hungary	0

SEMI-FINALS
| Brazil | 4 | Chile | 2 |
| Czechoslovakia | 3 | Yugoslavia | 1 |

THIRD-PLACE MATCH
| Chile | 1 | Yugoslavia | 0 |

Final – June 17: Nacional, Santiago
Brazil 3 (Amarildo 18, Zito 69, Vava 77)
Czechoslovakia 1 (Masopust 16)
HT: 1-1. **Att:** 68,679. **Ref:** Latishev (Soviet Union)
Brazil: Gilmar, D Santos, Mauro, Zozimo, N Santos, Zito, Didi, Zagallo, Garrincha, Vava, Amarildo.
Czechoslovakia: Schroiff ,Tichy, Pluskal, Popluhar, Novak, Kvasniak, Kadraba, Masopust, Pospichal, Scherer, Jelinek.
Top scorer: 4 Garrincha (Brazil), Vava (Brazil), L Sanchez (Chile), Jerkovic (Yugoslavia), Albert (Hungary), V Ivanov (Sov).

ENGLAND 1966

England became the third hosts to win the World Cup. Newcomers North Korea shocked Italy 1-0 in a group match and raced into a 3-0 quarter-final lead against highly-regarded Portugal, conquerors of an aged Brazil – Pele was again injured. But Golden Boot winner Eusebio converted two penalties and two other goals as Portugal won 5-3. In England's 1-0 quarter-final win at Wembley, Argentina's captain Antonio Rattin was dismissed and the players called animals by home coach Alf Ramsey. England beat Portugal in one semi-final, West Germany Russia in the other. And they produced a classic Final, which was only decided in the last seconds of extra time. For the fifth consecutive final, the scorers of the first goal lost, Helmut Haller having his strike cancelled out by Geoff Hurst. Martin Peters gave England the lead, only for Wolfgang Weber to equalise with almost the last kick of the 90 minutes. Hurst's controversial third goal was rendered moot when he completed his hat-trick.

GROUP 1

England	0		Uruguay	0			
France	1		Mexico	1			
Uruguay	2		France	1			
England	2		Mexico	0			
Uruguay	0		Mexico	0			
England	2		France	0			

	P	W	D	L	F	A	Pts
England	3	2	1	0	4	0	5
Uruguay	3	1	2	0	2	1	4
Mexico	3	0	2	1	1	3	2
France	3	0	1	2	2	5	1

GROUP 2

West Germany	5		Switzerland	0
Argentina	2		Spain	1
Spain	2		Switzerland	1
Argentina	0		West Germany	0
Argentina	2		Switzerland	0
West Germany	2		Spain	1

	P	W	D	L	F	A	Pts
West Germany	3	2	1	0	7	1	5
Argentina	3	2	1	0	4	1	5
Spain	3	1	0	2	4	5	2
Switzerland	3	0	0	3	1	9	0

GROUP 3

Brazil	2		Bulgaria	0
Portugal	3		Hungary	1
Hungary	3		Brazil	1
Portugal	3		Bulgaria	0
Portugal	3		Brazil	1
Hungary	3		Bulgaria	1

	P	W	D	L	F	A	Pts
Portugal	3	3	0	0	9	2	6
Hungary	3	2	0	1	7	5	4
Brazil	3	1	0	2	4	6	2
Bulgaria	3	0	0	3	1	8	0

GROUP 4

Soviet Union	3		North Korea	0
Italy	2		Chile	0
Chile	1		North Korea	1
Soviet Union	1		Italy	0
North Korea	1		Italy	0
Soviet Union	2		Chile	1

	P	W	D	L	F	A	Pts
Soviet Union	3	3	0	0	6	1	6
North Korea	3	1	1	1	2	4	3
Italy	3	1	0	2	2	2	2
Chile	3	0	1	2	2	5	1

QUARTER-FINALS

England	1		Argentina	0
West Germany	4		Uruguay	0
Portugal	5		North Korea	3
Soviet Union	2		Hungary	1

SEMI-FINALS

West Germany	2		Soviet Union	1
England	2		Portugal	1

THIRD-PLACE MATCH

Portugal	2		Soviet Union	1

FINAL – July 30: Wembley, London

*England 4 (Hurst 19, 100, 120, Peters 77)
West Germany 2 (Haller 13, Weber 89)
HT: 1-1. **90min:** 2-2. **Att:** 96,924. **Ref:** Dienst (Switzerland)
England: Banks, Cohen, J Charlton, Moore, Wilson, Ball, Stiles, R Charlton, Peters, Hurst, Hunt.
West Germany: Tilkowski, Hottges, Schulz, Weber, Schnellinger, Haller, Beckenbauer, Overath, Seeler, Held, Emmerich.
Top scorer: 9 Eusebio (Portugal)

* After extra time

MEXICO 1970

The high-altitude of Mexico forced players to slow down their tempo and this probably helped to set up possibly the most skilful finals ever staged. Brazil, the pass-masters of measured soccer, certainly profited and a fully-fit Pele, aided by Gerson, Tostao, Rivelino and goal-a-game Jairzinho – Garrincha's successor and the first man to score in every match including the Final – conquered all before them. England and Brazil played the match of the finals, in a first round group match which ended 1-0, most famous for Gordon Banks's "save of the century" from Pele. It meant England had a repeat of the 1966 Final at the last eight stage. This time West Germany took advantage of Banks's absence with a stomach illness to win 3-2, but they lost a magnificent semi-final, 4-3 after extra time, to Italy. In the Final at the Azteca Stadium, although Roberto Boninsegna made it 1-1 after Pele had scored Brazil's 100th World Cup finals goal, Gerson, Jairzinho and, spectacularly, Carlos Alberto rounded off a 4-1 victory.

GROUP 1

Mexico	0		Soviet Union	0
Belgium	3		El Salvador	0
Soviet Union	4		Belgium	1
Mexico	4		El Salvador	0
Soviet Union	2		El Salvador	0
Mexico	1		Belgium	0

	P	W	D	L	F	A	Pts
Soviet Union	3	2	1	0	6	1	5
Mexico	3	2	1	0	5	0	5
Belgium	3	1	0	2	4	5	2
El Salvador	3	0	0	3	0	9	0

GROUP 2

Uruguay	2		Israel	0
Italy	1		Sweden	0
Uruguay	0		Italy	0
Sweden	1		Israel	1
Sweden	1		Uruguay	0
Italy	0		Israel	0

	P	W	D	L	F	A	Pts
Italy	3	1	2	0	1	0	4
Uruguay	3	1	1	1	2	1	3
Sweden	3	1	1	1	2	2	3
Israel	3	0	2	1	1	3	2

GROUP 3

England	1		Romania	0
Brazil	4		Czechoslovakia	1
Romania	2		Czechoslovakia	1
Brazil	1		England	0
Brazil	3		Romania	2
England	1		Czechoslovakia	0

	P	W	D	L	F	A	Pts
Brazil	3	3	0	0	8	3	6
England	3	2	0	1	2	1	4
Romania	3	1	0	2	4	5	2
Czechoslovakia	3	0	0	3	2	7	0

GROUP 4

Peru	3		Bulgaria	2
West Germany	2		Morocco	1
Peru	3		Morocco	0
West Germany	5		Bulgaria	2
West Germany	3		Peru	1
Morocco	1		Bulgaria	1

	P	W	D	L	F	A	Pts
West Germany	3	3	0	0	10	4	6
Peru	3	2	0	1	7	5	4
Bulgaria	3	0	1	2	5	9	1
Morocco	3	0	1	2	2	6	1

QUARTER-FINALS

West Germany	3		England	2*
Brazil	4		Peru	2
Italy	4		Mexico	1
Uruguay	1		Soviet Union	0

* After extra time

SEMI-FINALS

Italy	4		West Germany	3*
Brazil	3		Uruguay	1

* After extra time

THIRD-PLACE MATCH

West Germany	1		Uruguay	0

FINAL – June 21: Azteca, Mexico City

Brazil 4 (Pele 18, Gerson 66, Jairzinho 71, Carlos Alberto 86)
Italy 1 (Boninsegna 37)
HT: 1-1. **Att:** 107,000. **Ref:** Glockner (East Germany)
Brazil: Felix, Carlos Alberto, Brito, Piazza, Everaldo, Clodoaldo, Gerson, Rivelino, Jairzinho, Tostao, Pele.
Italy: Albertosi, Facchetti, Cera, Burgnich, Rosato, Domenghini, Bertini (Juliano 75), De Sisti, Mazzola, Boninsegna. (Rivera 84), Riva.
Top scorer: 9 Müller (West Germany)

WEST GERMANY 1974

Hosts West Germany were the first winners of the new World Cup after Brazil had annexed the Jules Rimet trophy with their third win in 1970. West German club soccer had eclipsed the Dutch just before the finals and it was repeated on the national stage, although the Johan Cruyff inspired Dutchmen played the best football. Intrigue came in the group stage where East met West and the battle for German supremacy went the former's way. Brazil lost their crown as Holland toyed with them in the second round group stage, whilst West Germany strode through the other section to set up a dream Final, efficiency against flair. There were six members of European champions Bayern Munich in Germany's starting line-up and six present or former Ajax players in Holland's 11. The Germans hadn't touched the ball when Berti Vogts fouled Cruyff and Johan Neeskens converted the penalty. Paul Breitner replied with a Germany penalty and Gerd Müller grabbed the winner.

FIRST ROUND – GROUP 1

West Germany	1		Chile	0
East Germany	2		Australia	0
West Germany	3		Australia	0
East Germany	1		Chile	1
East Germany	1		West Germany	0
Chile	0		Australia	0

	P	W	D	L	F	A	Pts
East Germany	3	2	1	0	4	1	5
West Germany	3	2	0	1	4	1	4
Chile	3	0	2	1	1	2	2
Australia	3	0	1	2	0	5	1

FIRST ROUND – GROUP 2

Brazil	0		Yugoslavia	0
Scotland	2		Zaïre	0
Brazil	0		Scotland	0
Yugoslavia	9		Zaïre	0
Scotland	1		Yugoslavia	1
Brazil	3		Zaïre	0

	P	W	D	L	F	A	Pts
Yugoslavia	3	1	2	0	10	1	4
Brazil	3	1	2	0	3	0	4
Scotland	3	1	2	0	3	1	4
Zaïre	3	0	0	3	0	14	0

FIRST ROUND GROUP 3

Holland	2	Uruguay	0
Sweden	0	Bulgaria	0
Holland	0	Sweden	0
Bulgaria	1	Uruguay	1
Holland	4	Bulgaria	1
Sweden	3	Uruguay	0

	P	W	D	L	F	A	Pts
Holland	3	2	1	0	6	1	5
Sweden	3	1	2	0	3	0	4
Bulgaria	3	0	2	1	2	5	2
Uruguay	3	0	1	2	1	6	1

FIRST ROUND – GROUP 4

Italy	3	Haiti	1
Poland	3	Argentina	2
Italy	1	Argentina	1
Poland	7	Haiti	0
Argentina	4	Haiti	1
Poland	2	Italy	1

	P	W	D	L	F	A	Pts
Poland	3	3	0	0	12	3	6
Argentina	3	1	1	1	7	5	3
Italy	3	1	1	1	5	4	3
Haiti	3	0	0	3	2	14	0

SECOND ROUND – GROUP A

Brazil	1	East Germany	0
Holland	4	Argentina	0
Holland	2	East Germany	0
Brazil	2	Argentina	1
Holland	2	Brazil	0
Argentina	1	East Germany	1

	P	W	D	L	F	A	Pts
Holland	3	3	0	0	8	0	6
Brazil	3	2	0	1	3	3	4
East Germany	3	0	1	2	1	4	1
Argentina	3	0	1	2	2	7	1

SECOND ROUND – GROUP B

Poland	1	Sweden	0
West Germany	2	Yugoslavia	0
Poland	2	Yugoslavia	1
West Germany	4	Sweden	2
Sweden	2	Yugoslavia	1
West Germany	1	Poland	0

	P	W	D	L	F	A	Pts
West Germany	3	3	0	0	7	2	6
Poland	3	2	0	1	3	2	4
Sweden	3	1	0	2	4	6	2
Yugoslavia	3	0	0	3	2	6	0

THIRD-PLACE MATCH

Poland	1	Brazil	0

FINAL – July 7: Olympia, Munich

West Germany 2 (Breitner 25 pen, Müller 43)
Holland 1 (Neeskens 2 pen)
HT: 2-1. **Att:** 77,833. **Ref:** Taylor (England).
West Germany: Maier, Vogts, Schwarzenbeck, Beckenbauer, Breitner, Bonhof, Hoeness, Overath, Grabowski, Müller, Holzenbein.
Holland: Jongbloed, Suurbier, Rijsbergen (De Jong 69), Haan, Krol, Jansen, Neeskens, Van Hanegem, Cruyff, Rep, Rensenbrink (R Van de Kerkhof 46).
Top scorer: 7 Lato (Poland)

ARGENTINA 1978

Argentina's repressive politicians were unloved around the world but they did manage to get the organisation and infrastructure in place for the 1978 finals. Coach Cesar Luis Menotti omitted teenage sensation Diego Maradona and selected 21 home-based players in Argentina's squad, the exception being Valencia's Mario Kempes. Britain's only representatives, for the second straight finals, were Scotland and although they went home after the first round, they had the consolation of Archie Gemmell scoring the goal of the tournament in a 3-2 defeat of Holland. The Dutch, even without Johan Cruyff, made it back to the Final, but they again lost to the hosts. Kempes opened the scoring and restored the Argentine lead in extra-time, sandwiching Dirk Naninga's goal for Holland. Daniel Bertoni made it 3-1 late on, and on a tickertape covered pitch, Argentina celebrated a first World Cup success.

FIRST ROUND – GROUP 1

Argentina	2	Hungary	1
Italy	2	France	1
Argentina	2	France	1
Italy	3	Hungary	1
Italy	1	Argentina	0
France	3	Hungary	1

	P	W	D	L	F	A	Pts
Italy	3	3	0	0	6	2	6
Argentina	3	2	0	1	4	3	4
France	3	1	0	2	5	5	2
Hungary	3	0	0	3	3	8	0

FIRST ROUND – GROUP 2

West Germany	0	Poland	0
Tunisia	3	Mexico	1
Poland	1	Tunisia	0
West Germany	6	Mexico	0
Poland	3	Mexico	1
West Germany	0	Tunisia	0

	P	W	D	L	F	A	Pts
Poland	3	2	1	0	4	1	5
West Germany	3	1	2	0	6	0	4
Tunisia	3	1	1	1	3	2	3
Mexico	3	0	0	3	2	12	0

FIRST ROUND – GROUP 3

Austria	2	Spain	1
Sweden	1	Brazil	1
Austria	1	Sweden	0
Brazil	0	Spain	0
Spain	1	Sweden	0
Brazil	1	Austria	0

	P	W	D	L	F	A	Pts
Austria	3	2	0	1	3	2	4
Brazil	3	1	2	0	2	1	4
Spain	3	1	1	1	2	2	3
Sweden	3	0	1	2	1	3	1

FIRST ROUND – GROUP 4

Peru	3	Scotland	1
Holland	3	Iran	0
Scotland	1	Iran	1
Holland	0	Peru	0
Peru	4	Iran	1
Scotland	3	Holland	2

	P	W	D	L	F	A	Pts
Peru	3	2	1	0	7	2	5
Holland	3	1	1	1	5	3	3
Scotland	3	1	1	1	5	6	3
Iran	3	0	1	2	2	8	1

SECOND ROUND – GROUP A

Italy	0	West Germany	0
Holland	5	Austria	1
Italy	1	Austria	0
Austria	3	West Germany	2
Holland	2	Italy	1
Holland	2	West Germany	2

	P	W	D	L	F	A	Pts
Holland	3	2	1	0	9	4	5
Italy	3	1	1	1	2	2	3
West Germany	3	0	2	1	4	5	2
Austria	3	1	0	2	4	8	2

SECOND ROUND – GROUP B

Argentina	2	Poland	0
Brazil	3	Peru	0
Argentina	0	Brazil	0
Poland	1	Peru	0
Brazil	3	Poland	1
Argentina	6	Peru	0

	P	W	D	L	F	A	Pts
Argentina	3	2	1	0	8	0	5
Brazil	3	2	1	0	6	1	5
Poland	3	1	0	2	2	5	2
Peru	3	0	0	3	0	10	0

THIRD-PLACE MATCH

Brazil	2	Italy	1

FINAL – June 25: Monumental, Buenos Aires

*Argentina 3 (Kempes 37, 104, Bertoni 114)
Holland 1 (Nanninga 81)
HT: 1-0. **90min:** 1-1. **Att:** 77,260. **Ref:** Gonella (Italy).
Argentina: Fillol, Olguin, Galvan, Passarella, Tarantini, Ardiles (Larrosa 66), Gallego, Bertoni, Kempes, Ortiz (Houseman 75), Luque.
Holland: Jongbloed, Krol, Poortvliet, Brandts, Jansen (Suurbier 73), R Van de Kerkhof, Neeskens, W Van de Kerkhof, Haan, Rep (Nanninga 59), Rensenbrink.
Top scorer: 6 Kempes (Argentina)

* After extra time

SPAIN 1982

Italy joined Brazil as three-time World Cup winners with a spectacular turnaround in form. After drawing all three first round group matches, including with newcomers Cameroon, they were superb in the second round group, beating Argentina 2-1 and Brazil 3-2. Their hero was Paolo Rossi – just back after an 18-month ban – who grabbed a hat-trick. Hosts Spain limped into the second stage despite losing to Northern Ireland, but lost to West Germany and drew with England, so couldn't become a third straight home champion. Two terrible assaults marred the latter stages: Diego Maradona kicked Brazil's Batista in the lower abdomen and West German goalkeeper Harald Schumacher broke the neck of France's Patrick Battiston in the semi-final. Germany triumphed in the first ever World Cup penalty shoot-out, but lost 3-1 in the Final. Despite a penalty miss by Antonio Cabrini, second-half goals from Rossi, Marco Tardelli and Alessandro Altobelli came before Paul Breitner scored his second World Cup Final penalty.

FIRST ROUND – GROUP 1

Italy	0	Poland	0
Peru	0	Cameroon	0
Italy	1	Peru	1
Poland	0	Cameroon	0
Poland	5	Peru	1
Italy	1	Cameroon	1

	P	W	D	L	F	A	Pts
Poland	3	1	2	0	5	1	4
Italy	3	0	3	0	2	2	3
Cameroon	3	0	3	0	1	1	3
Peru	3	0	2	1	2	6	2

FIRST ROUND – GROUP 2

Algeria	2	West Germany	1
Austria	1	Chile	0
West Germany	4	Chile	1
Austria	2	Algeria	0
Algeria	3	Chile	2
West Germany	1	Austria	0

	P	W	D	L	F	A	Pts
West Germany	3	2	0	1	6	3	4
Austria	3	2	0	1	3	1	4
Algeria	3	2	0	1	5	5	4
Chile	3	0	0	3	3	8	0

FIRST ROUND – GROUP 3

Belgium	1	Argentina	0
Hungary	10	El Salvador	1
Argentina	4	Hungary	1
Belgium	1	El Salvador	0
Belgium	1	Hungary	1
Argentina	2	El Salvador	0

	P	W	D	L	F	A	Pts
Belgium	3	2	1	0	3	1	5
Argentina	3	2	0	1	6	2	4
Hungary	3	1	1	1	12	6	3
El Salvador	3	0	0	3	1	13	3

FIRST ROUND – GROUP 4

England	3	France	1
Czechoslovakia	1	Kuwait	1
England	2	Czechoslovakia	0
France	4	Kuwait	1
France	1	Czechoslovakia	1
England	1	Kuwait	0

	P	W	D	L	F	A	Pts
England	3	3	0	0	6	1	6
France	3	1	1	1	6	5	3
Czechoslovakia	3	0	2	1	2	4	2
Kuwait	3	0	1	2	2	6	1

FIRST ROUND – GROUP 5

Spain	1	Honduras	1
Northern Ireland	0	Yugoslavia	0
Spain	2	Yugoslavia	1
Northern Ireland	1	Honduras	1
Yugoslavia	1	Honduras	0
Northern Ireland	1	Spain	0

	P	W	D	L	F	A	Pts
N. Ireland	3	1	2	0	2	1	4
Spain	3	1	1	1	3	3	3
Yugoslavia	3	1	1	1	2	2	3
Honduras	3	0	2	1	2	3	2

FIRST ROUND – GROUP 6

Brazil	2	Soviet Union	1
Scotland	5	New Zealand	2
Brazil	4	Scotland	1
Soviet Union	3	New Zealand	0
Scotland	2	Soviet Union	2
Brazil	4	New Zealand	0

	P	W	D	L	F	A	Pts
Brazil	3	3	0	0	10	2	6
Soviet Union	3	1	1	1	6	4	3
Scotland	3	1	1	1	8	8	3
New Zealand	3	0	0	3	2	12	0

SECOND ROUND – GROUP A

Poland	3	Belgium	0
Soviet Union	1	Belgium	0
Soviet Union	0	Poland	0

	P	W	D	L	F	A	Pts
Poland	2	1	1	0	3	0	3
Soviet Union	2	1	1	0	1	0	3
Belgium	2	0	0	2	0	4	0

SECOND ROUND – GROUP B

West Germany	0	England	0
West Germany	2	Spain	1
England	0	Spain	0

	P	W	D	L	F	A	Pts
West Germany	2	1	1	0	2	1	3
England	2	0	2	0	0	0	2
Spain	2	0	1	1	1	2	1

SECOND ROUND – GROUP C

Italy	2	Argentina	1
Brazil	3	Argentina	1
Italy	3	Brazil	2

	P	W	D	L	F	A	Pts
Italy	2	2	0	0	5	3	4
Brazil	2	1	0	1	5	4	2
Argentina	2	0	0	2	2	5	0

SECOND ROUND – GROUP D

France	1	Austria	0
Northern Ireland	2	Austria	2
France	4	Northern Ireland	1

	P	W	D	L	F	A	Pts
France	2	2	0	0	5	1	4
Austria	2	0	1	1	2	3	1
N.Ireland	2	0	1	1	3	6	1

SEMI-FINALS

Italy	2	Poland	0
West Germany	3 (5)	France	3 (4)*

After extra time (pens)

THIRD-PLACE MATCH

Poland	3	France	2

FINAL – July 11: Bernabeu, Madrid

Italy 3 (Rossi 56, Tardelli 69, Altobelli 80) **West Germany 1** (Breitner 82)
HT: 0-0. **Att:** 90,000. **Ref:** Coelho (Brazil).
Italy: Zoff, Scirea, Bergomi, Gentile, Collovati, Cabrini, Oriale, Tardelli, Conti, Graziani (Altobelli 8; Causio 88), Rossi. **West Germany:** Schumacher, Kaltz, K Forster, Stielike, B Forster, Breitner, Dremmler (Hrubesch 63), Briegel, Littbarski, Fischer, Rummenigge (H Muller 70).
Top scorer: 6 Rossi (Italy)

MEXICO 1986

Mexico stepped in to replace Colombia as hosts for 1986 – the first country to stage two World Cup finals – but they lost a quarter-final shoot-out against West Germany. The hero and villain of the finals was Diego Maradona. Argentina scored 14 goals on their way to winning their second World Cup and the captain scored five of them and created another five. In the Final against West Germany, despite being almost marked out of the game by Lothar Matthäus, with five minutes to go, he set up Jorge Burruchaga for the winning goal. Another world superstar, Michel Platini, helped to end Brazil's interest with an equalising penalty, but he missed in the quarter-final shoot-out, which France nonetheless won – an eventful 31st birthday. Pat Jennings' 40th birthday was less successful. His final international ended in Northern Ireland's 3-0 loss to Brazil. But the 1986 finals cannot be mentioned without Maradona's "Hand of God" and magical goals two minutes apart as England lost 2-1 in the quarter-final. Golden Boot winner Gary Lineker netted for England.

FIRST ROUND – GROUP A

Bulgaria	1	Italy	1
Argentina	3	South Korea	1
Italy	1	Argentina	1
Bulgaria	1	South Korea	1
Argentina	2	Bulgaria	0
Italy	3	South Korea	2

	P	W	D	L	F	A	Pts
Argentina	3	2	1	0	6	2	5
Italy	3	1	2	0	5	4	4
Bulgaria	3	0	2	1	2	4	2
South Korea	3	0	1	2	4	7	1

FIRST ROUND – GROUP B

Mexico	2	Belgium	1
Paraguay	1	Iraq	0
Mexico	1	Paraguay	1
Belgium	2	Iraq	1
Paraguay	2	Belgium	2
Mexico	1	Iraq	0

	P	W	D	L	F	A	Pts
Mexico	3	2	1	0	4	2	5
Paraguay	3	1	2	0	4	3	4
Belgium	3	1	1	1	5	5	3
Iraq	3	0	0	3	1	4	0

FIRST ROUND – GROUP C

Soviet Union	6	Hungary	0
France	1	Canada	0
Soviet Union	1	France	1
Hungary	2	Canada	0
France	3	Hungary	0
Soviet Union	2	Canada	0

	P	W	D	L	F	A	Pts
Soviet Union	3	2	1	0	9	1	5
France	3	2	1	0	5	1	5
Hungary	3	1	0	2	2	9	2
Canada	3	0	0	3	0	5	0

FIRST ROUND – GROUP D

Brazil	1	Spain	0
Northern Ireland	1	Algeria	1
Spain	2	Northern Ireland	1
Brazil	1	Algeria	0
Spain	3	Algeria	0
Brazil	3	Northern Ireland	0

	P	W	D	L	F	A	Pts
Brazil	3	3	0	0	5	0	6
Spain	3	2	0	1	5	2	4
N.Ireland	3	0	1	2	2	6	1
Algeria	3	0	1	2	1	5	1

SECOND ROUND – GROUP E

West Germany	1	Uruguay	1
Denmark	1	Scotland	0
Denmark	6	Uruguay	1
West Germany	2	Scotland	1
Scotland	0	Uruguay	0
Denmark	2	West Germany	0

	P	W	D	L	F	A	Pts
Denmark	3	3	0	0	9	1	6
West Germany	3	1	1	1	3	4	3
Uruguay	3	0	2	1	2	7	2
Scotland	3	0	1	2	1	3	1

SECOND ROUND – GROUP F

Morocco	0	Poland	0
Portugal	1	England	0
England	0	Morocco	0
Poland	1	Portugal	0
England	3	Poland	0
Morocco	3	Portugal	1

	P	W	D	L	F	A	Pts
Morocco	3	1	2	0	3	1	4
England	3	1	1	1	3	1	3
Poland	3	1	1	1	1	3	3
Portugal	3	1	0	2	2	4	2

SECOND ROUND

Mexico	2	Bulgaria	0
Belgium	4	Soviet Union	3*
Brazil	4	Poland	0
Argentina	1	Uruguay	0
France	2	Italy	0
West Germany	1	Morocco	0
England	3	Paraguay	0
Spain	5	Denmark	1

After extra time

QUARTER-FINALS

France	1 (4)	Brazil	1 (3)*
West Germany	0 (4)	Mexico	0 (1)*
Argentina	2	England	1
Spain	1 (5)	Belgium	1 (4)*

After extra time (pens)

SEMI-FINALS

Argentina	2	Belgium	0
West Germany	2	France	0

THIRD-PLACE MATCH

France	4	Belgium	2

FINAL – June 29: Azteca, Mexico City

Argentina 3 (Brown 22, Valdano 56, Burruchaga 84)
West Germany 2 (Rummenigge 73, Völler 82)
HT: 1-0. **Att:** 114,590. **Ref:** Arppi Filho (Brazil).
Argentina: Pumpido, Cuciuffo, Brown, Ruggeri, Giusti, Burruchaga (Trobbiani 89), Batista, Enrique, Olarticoechea, Maradona, Valdano.
West Germany: Schumacher, Berthold, Jakobs, Forster, Eder, Brehme, Matthaus, Magath (D Hoeness 63), Briegel, Allofs (Völler 46), Rummenigge.
Top scorer: 6 Lineker (England).

ITALY 1990

Sadly most of the passion at Italia 90 was found in the atmosphere in the stands rather than on the pitch. Franz Beckenbauer became the first man to captain and coach World Cup winners as West Germany avenged their 1986 defeat in a spiteful Final. Andy Brehme converted a penalty after 85 minutes of a match which saw the first ever red cards in a Final, shown by referee Mendez to Pedro Monzon and Gustavo Dezotti. Argentina had opened the finals with a shock 1-0 defeat by Cameroon, and the Africans finished with nine men after two dismissals. Instead of Diego Maradona, Argentina's hero of the tournament was goalkeeper Sergio Goycochea, who made crucial saves in penalty shoot-out victories over Yugoslavia in the second round and Italy in the semi-final. England stuttered and stumbled, but still managed to reach the semi-finals, where they lost on penalties to the Germans. At least hosts the had the consolation of finishing third and having the Golden Boot winner in "Toto" Schillaci.

GROUP A

Italy	1	Austria	0
Czechoslovakia	5	USA	1
Italy	1	USA	0
Czechoslovakia	1	Austria	0
Italy	2	Czechoslovakia	0
Austria	2	USA	1

	P	W	D	L	F	A	Pts
Italy	3	3	0	0	4	0	6
Czechoslovakia	3	2	0	1	6	3	4
Austria	3	1	0	2	2	3	2
USA	3	0	0	3	2	8	0

GROUP B

Cameroon	1	Argentina	0
Romania	2	Soviet Union	0
Argentina	2	Soviet Union	0
Cameroon	2	Romania	1
Argentina	1	Romania	1
Soviet Union	4	Cameroon	0

	P	W	D	L	F	A	Pts
Cameroon	3	2	0	1	3	5	4
Romania	3	1	1	1	4	3	3
Argentina	3	1	1	1	3	2	3
Soviet Union	3	1	0	2	4	4	2

GROUP C

Brazil	2	Sweden	1
Costa Rica	1	Scotland	0
Brazil	1	Costa Rica	0
Scotland	2	Sweden	1
Brazil	1	Scotland	0
Costa Rica	2	Sweden	1

	P	W	D	L	F	A	Pts
Brazil	3	3	0	0	4	1	6
Costa Rica	3	2	0	1	3	2	4
Scotland	3	1	0	2	2	3	2
Sweden	3	0	0	3	3	6	0

GROUP D

Colombia	2	UAE	0
West Germany	4	Yugoslavia	1
Yugoslavia	1	Colombia	0
West Germany	5	UAE	1
West Germany	1	Colombia	1
Yugoslavia	4	UAE	1

	P	W	D	L	F	A	Pts
West Germany	3	2	1	0	10	3	5
Yugoslavia	3	2	0	1	6	5	4
Colombia	3	1	1	1	3	2	3
UAE	3	0	0	3	2	11	0

GROUP E

Belgium	2	South Korea	0
Uruguay	0	Spain	0
Belgium	3	Uruguay	1
Spain	3	South Korea	1
Spain	2	Belgium	1
Uruguay	1	South Korea	0

	P	W	D	L	F	A	Pts
Spain	3	2	1	0	5	2	5
Belgium	3	2	0	1	6	3	4
Uruguay	3	1	1	1	2	3	3
South Korea	3	0	0	3	1	6	0

GROUP F

England	1	Rep. of Ireland	1
Holland	1	Egypt	1
England	0	Holland	0
Egypt	0	Rep. of Ireland	0
England	1	Egypt	0
Holland	1	Rep. of Ireland	1

	P	W	D	L	F	A	Pts
England	3	1	2	0	2	1	4
Rep. of Ireland	3	0	3	0	2	2	3
Holland	3	0	3	0	2	2	3
Egypt	3	0	2	1	1	2	2

SECOND ROUND

Cameroon	2	Colombia	1*
Czechoslovakia	4	Costa Rica	1
Argentina	1	Brazil	0
West Germany	2	Holland	1
Rep. of Ireland	0 (5)	Romania	0 (4)*
Italy	2	Uruguay	0
Yugoslavia	2	Spain	1*
England	1	Belgium	0*

After extra time (pens)

QUARTER-FINALS

Argentina	0 (3)	Yugoslavia	0 (2)*
Italy	1	Rep of Ireland	0
West Germany	1	Czechoslovakia	0
England	3	Cameroon	2*

After extra time (pens)

SEMI-FINALS

Argentina	1 (4)	Italy	1 (3)*
West Germany	1 (4)	England	1 (3)*

After extra time (pens)

THIRD-PLACE MATCH

Italy	2	England	1

FINAL – July 8: Olimpico, Rome

West Germany 1 (Brehme 84 pen)
Argentina 0
HT: 0-0. **Att:** 73,603. **Ref:** Codesal (Mexico)
West Germany: Illgner, Berthold (Reuter 74), Kohler, Augenthaler, Brehme, Hassler, Buchwald, Matthaus, Littbarski, Völler, Klinsmann.
Argentina: Goycochea, Lorenzo, Ruggeri (Monzon 46), Serrizuela, Sensini, Simon, Basualdo, Burruchaga (Calderon 53), Maradona, Troglio, Dezotti.
Sent off: Monzon, Dezotti.
Top scorer: 6 Schillaci (Italy)

USA 1994

Purists were unhappy that the USA was awarded the World Cup, but they were enthusiastic hosts. The tournament attracted record crowds and FIFA's tough policy on foul play made the soccer more watchable. Controversy and Diego Maradona go hand in hand and so it was in 1994, when he was sent home in disgrace after a failed drugs test. Also going home early was Germany's Steffen Effenberg, for a rude gesture to German fans. Worst of all, Andres Escobar, who had scored an unfortunate own goal in Colombia's 2-1 loss to the hosts, was gunned down at his home five days after his country's exit. The surprise team was Bulgaria, who won their first finals match and reached the semi-finals. Brazil won their fourth World Cup, though the Final against Italy was a dull goalless draw decided by the first Final penalty shoot-out.

GROUP A

USA	1	Switzerland	1
Colombia	1	Romania	3
USA	2	Colombia	1
Romania	1	Switzerland	4
USA	0	Romania	1
Switzerland	0	Colombia	2

	P	W	D	L	F	A	Pts
Romania	3	2	0	1	5	5	6
Switzerland	3	1	1	1	5	4	4
USA	3	1	1	1	3	3	4
Colombia	3	1	0	2	4	5	3

GROUP B

Cameroon	2	Sweden	2
Brazil	2	Russia	0
Brazil	3	Cameroon	0
Sweden	3	Russia	1
Russia	6	Cameroon	1
Brazil	1	Sweden	1

	P	W	D	L	F	A	Pts
Brazil	3	2	1	0	6	1	7
Sweden	3	1	2	0	6	4	5
Russia	3	1	0	2	7	6	3
Cameroon	3	0	1	2	3	11	1

GROUP C

Germany	1	Bolivia	0
Spain	2	South Korea	2
Germany	1	Spain	1
South Korea	0	Bolivia	0
Bolivia	1	Spain	3
Germany	3	South Korea	2

	P	W	D	L	F	A	Pts
Germany	3	2	1	0	5	3	7
Spain	3	1	2	0	6	4	5
South Korea	3	0	2	1	4	5	2
Bolivia	3	0	1	2	1	4	1

GROUP D

Argentina	4	Greece	0
Nigeria	3	Bulgaria	0
Argentina	2	Nigeria	1
Bulgaria	4	Greece	0
Greece	0	Nigeria	2
Argentina	0	Bulgaria	2

	P	W	D	L	F	A	Pts
Nigeria	3	2	0	1	6	2	6
Bulgaria	3	2	0	1	6	3	6
Argentina	3	2	0	1	6	3	6
Greece	3	0	0	3	0	10	0

GROUP E

Italy	0	Rep. of Ireland	1
Norway	1	Mexico	0
Italy	1	Norway	0
Mexico	2	Rep. of Ireland	1
Rep. of Ireland	0	Norway	0
Italy	1	Mexico	1

	P	W	D	L	F	A	Pts
Mexico	3	1	1	1	3	3	4
Rep. of Ireland	3	1	1	1	2	2	4
Italy	3	1	1	1	2	2	4
Norway	3	1	1	1	1	1	4

GROUP F

Belgium	1	Morocco	0
Holland	2	Saudi Arabia	1
Belgium	1	Holland	0
Saudi Arabia	2	Morocco	1
Morocco	1	Holland	2
Belgium	0	Saudi Arabia	1

	P	W	D	L	F	A	Pts
Holland	3	2	0	1	4	3	6
Saudi Arabia	3	2	0	1	4	3	6
Belgium	3	2	0	1	2	1	6
Morocco	3	0	0	3	2	5	0

SECOND ROUND

Germany	3	Belgium	2
Spain	3	Switzerland	0
Sweden	3	Saudi Arabia	1
Romania	3	Argentina	2
Holland	2	Rep. of Ireland	0
Brazil	1	USA	0
Italy	2	Nigeria	1*
Bulgaria	1(3)	Mexico	1 (1)*

After extra time (pens)

QUARTER-FINALS

Italy	2	Spain	1
Brazil	3	Holland	2
Bulgaria	2	Germany	1
Sweden	2 (5)	Romania	2 (4)*

After extra time (pens)

SEMI-FINALS

Brazil	1	Sweden	0
Italy	2	Bulgaria	1

THIRD-PLACE MATCH

Sweden	4	Bulgaria	0

FINAL – July 17: Rose Bowl, Pasadena

Brazil 0 (3)
Italy 0 (2)*
HT: 0-0. **Att:** 94,000. **Ref:** Puhl (Hungary)
Brazil: Taffarel, Jorginho (Cafu 20), Aldair, Marcio Santos, Branco, Mazinho, Dunga, Mauro Silva, Zinho (Viola 106), Romario, Bebeto.
Italy: Pagliuca, Mussi (Apolloni 34), Maldini, Baresi, Benarrivo, Donadoni, Berti, Albertini, D Baggio (Evani 94), R Baggio, Massaro.
Top scorer: 6 Salenko (Russia), Stoichkov (Bulgaria).
After extra time (pens)

FRANCE 1998

France, the birthplace of FIFA and Jules Rimet, the founder of the World Cup, hosted the last finals of the 20th century and the country celebrated with more than a million fans lining the Champs Elysées after the 3-0 defeat of Brazil in the Final. Coach Aime Jacquet, under pressure before the finals for his and his Federation's belief in youth academies, became a national hero as did French-Algerian Zinedine Zidane, who netted twice in the Final – Emmanuel Petit scored the other. It seemed like a thousand years after Zidane's red card and two-match suspension in the group stage. England again lost on penalties to a nemesis, this time Argentina, after a thrilling 2-2 draw in St Etienne. As great as teenager Michael Owen's spectacular goal was, David Beckham's red card for kicking out at wily veteran Diego Simeone attracted all the headlines. Croatia's first finals ended with third place and the Golden Boot winner in Davor Suker. French captain Laurent Blanc scored the World Cup's first ever extra-time golden goal, breaking a goalless deadlock against Paraguay in the second round.

GROUP A

Brazil	2	Scotland					1
Morocco	2	Norway					2
Brazil	3	Morocco					0
Scotland	1	Norway					1
Brazil	1	Norway					2
Scotland	0	Morocco					3

	P	W	D	L	F	A	Pts
Brazil	3	2	0	1	6	3	6
Norway	3	1	2	0	5	4	5
Morocco	3	1	1	1	5	5	4
Scotland	3	0	1	2	2	6	1

GROUP B

Italy	2	Chile	2
Austria	1	Cameroon	1
Chile	1	Austria	1
Italy	3	Cameroon	0
Chile	1	Cameroon	1
Italy	2	Austria	1

	P	W	D	L	F	A	Pts
Italy	3	2	1	0	7	3	7
Chile	3	0	3	0	4	4	3
Austria	3	0	2	1	3	4	2
Cameroon	3	0	2	1	2	5	2

GROUP C

Saudi Arabia	0	Denmark	1
France	3	South Africa	0
France	4	Saudi Arabia	0
South Africa	1	Denmark	1
France	2	Denmark	1
South Africa	2	Saudi Arabia	2

	P	W	D	L	F	A	Pts
France	3	3	0	0	9	1	9
Denmark	3	1	1	1	3	3	4
S. Africa	3	0	2	1	3	6	2
S. Arabia	3	0	1	2	2	7	1

GROUP D

Paraguay	0	Bulgaria	0
Spain	2	Nigeria	3
Nigeria	1	Bulgaria	0
Spain	0	Paraguay	0
Nigeria	1	Paraguay	3
Spain	6	Bulgaria	1

	P	W	D	L	F	A	Pts
Nigeria	3	2	0	1	5	5	6
Paraguay	3	1	2	0	3	1	5
Spain	3	1	1	1	8	4	5
Bulgaria	3	0	1	2	1	7	1

GROUP E

South Korea	1	Mexico	3
Holland	0	Belgium	0
Belgium	2	Mexico	2
Holland	5	South Korea	0
Belgium	1	South Korea	1
Holland	2	Mexico	2

	P	W	D	L	F	A	Pts
Holland	3	1	2	0	7	2	5
Mexico	3	1	2	0	7	5	5
Belgium	3	0	3	0	3	3	3
South Korea	3	0	1	2	2	9	1

GROUP F

Germany	2	USA	0
Yugoslavia	1	Iran	0
Germany	2	Yugoslavia	2
USA	1	Iran	2
Germany	2	Iran	0
USA	0	Yugoslavia	1

	P	W	D	L	F	A	Pts
Germany	3	2	1	0	6	2	7
Yugoslavia	3	2	1	0	4	2	7
Iran	3	1	0	2	2	4	3
USA	3	0	0	3	1	5	0

GROUP G

England	2	Tunisia	0
Romania	1	Colombia	0
Colombia	1	Tunisia	0
Romania	2	England	1
Romania	1	Tunisia	1
Colombia	0	England	2

	P	W	D	L	F	A	Pts
Romania	3	2	1	0	4	2	7
England	3	2	0	1	5	2	6
Colombia	3	1	0	2	1	3	3
Tunisia	3	0	1	2	1	4	1

GROUP H

Argentina	1	Japan	0
Jamaica	1	Croatia	3
Japan	0	Croatia	1
Argentina	5	Jamaica	0
Argentina	1	Croatia	0
Japan	1	Jamaica	2

	P	W	D	L	F	A	Pts
Argentina	3	3	0	0	7	0	9
Croatia	3	2	0	1	4	2	6
Jamaica	3	1	0	2	3	9	3
Japan	3	0	0	3	1	5	0

SECOND ROUND

Italy	1	Norway	0
Brazil	4	Chile	1
France	0 [1]	Paraguay	0 *
Nigeria	1	Denmark	4
Germany	2	Mexico	1
Holland	2	Yugoslavia	1
Romania	0	Croatia	1
Argentina	2 (4)	England	2 (3)*

* After extra time (pens) [golden goal]

QUARTER-FINALS

Italy	0 (3)	France	0 (4)*
Brazil	3	Denmark	2
Holland	2	Argentina	1
Germany	0	Croatia	3

* After extra time (pens)

SEMI-FINALS

Brazil	1 (4)	Holland	1 (2)*
France	2	Croatia	1

* After extra time (pens)

THIRD-PLACE MATCH

Holland	1	Croatia	2

FINAL – July 12: Stade de France, Paris

France 3 (Zidane 27, 45, Petit 90)
Brazil 0
HT: 1-0. **Att:** 75,000. **Ref:** Belqola (Morocco)
France: Barthez, Thuram, Leboeuf, Desailly, Lizarazu, Petit, Deschamps, Karembeu (Boghossian 58), Zidane, Guivarc'h (Dugarry 66), Djorkaeff (Vieira 76). **Sent off:** Desailly.
Brazil: Taffarel, Cafu, Junior Baiano, Aldair, Roberto Carlos, Dunga, Cesar Sampaio (Edmundo 75), Leonardo (Denilson 46), Rivaldo, Bebeto, Ronaldo.
Top scorer: 6 Suker (Croatia)

SOUTH KOREA/JAPAN 2002

Ronaldo's nightmare end to the 1998 finals was forgotten as he won the Golden Boot and scored his seventh and eighth goals as Brazil defeated Germany 2–0 in the Final to win their fifth World Cup. Co-hosts Japan and South Korea did surprisingly well, Japan reaching the second round and South Korea the semi-final. Argentina went out in the first round after losing to England on a David Beckham penalty. Germany and Turkey apart, European countries fared badly. Holders France lost the opening game 1–0 to Senegal and went home after failing to score a single goal – a feat matched by debutants China – and neither Portugal nor Croatia reached the second round. In the knock-out stages, both Spain – conquerors of the Republic of Ireland – and Italy fell to the Guus Hiddink-coached Koreans. England lost in the blazing heat of Shizuoka to Brazil in the quarter-final where Ronaldinho scored and was later sent off.

GROUP A

Senegal	1	France	0
Denmark	2	Uruguay	1
France	0	Uruguay	0
Denmark	1	Senegal	1
Denmark	2	France	0
Senegal	3	Uruguay	3

	P	W	D	L	F	A	Pts
Denmark	3	2	1	0	5	2	7
Senegal	3	1	2	0	5	4	5
Uruguay	3	0	2	1	4	5	2
France	3	0	1	2	0	3	1

GROUP B

Paraguay	2	South Africa	2
Spain	3	Slovenia	1
Spain	3	Paraguay	1
South Africa	1	Slovenia	0
Spain	3	South Africa	2
Paraguay	3	Slovenia	1

	P	W	D	L	F	A	Pts
Spain	3	3	0	0	9	4	9
Paraguay	3	1	1	1	6	6	4
South Africa	3	1	1	1	5	5	4
Slovenia	3	0	0	3	2	7	0

GROUP C

Brazil	2	Turkey	1
Costa Rica	2	China	0
Brazil	4	China	0
Costa Rica	1	Turkey	1
Brazil	5	Costa Rica	2
Turkey	3	China	0

	P	W	D	L	F	A	Pts
Brazil	3	3	0	0	11	3	9
Turkey	3	1	1	1	5	3	4
Costa Rica	3	1	1	1	5	6	4
China	3	0	0	3	0	9	0

GROUP D

South Korea	2	Poland	0
USA	3	Portugal	2
South Korea	1	USA	1
Portugal	4	Poland	0
South Korea	1	Portugal	0
Poland	3	USA	1

	P	W	D	L	F	A	Pts
South Korea	3	2	1	0	4	1	7
USA	3	1	1	1	5	6	4
Portugal	3	1	0	2	6	4	3
Poland	3	1	0	2	3	7	3

GROUP E

Rep. of Ireland	1	Cameroon	1
Germany	8	Saudi Arabia	0
Germany	1	Rep. of Ireland	1
Cameroon	1	Saudi Arabia	0
Germany	2	Cameroon	0
Rep. of Ireland	3	Saudi Arabia	0

	P	W	D	L	F	A	Pts
Germany	3	2	1	0	11	1	7
Rep. Ireland	3	1	2	0	5	2	5
Cameroon	3	1	1	1	2	3	4
Saudi Arabia	3	0	0	3	0	12	0

GROUP F

England	1	Sweden	1
Argentina	1	Nigeria	0
Sweden	2	Nigeria	1
England	1	Argentina	0
Sweden	1	Argentina	1
Nigeria	0	England	0

	P	W	D	L	F	A	Pts
Sweden	3	1	2	0	4	3	5
England	3	1	2	0	2	1	5
Argentina	3	1	1	1	2	2	4
Nigeria	3	0	1	2	1	3	1

GROUP G

Mexico	1	Croatia	0
Italy	2	Ecuador	0
Croatia	2	Italy	1
Mexico	2	Ecuador	1
Mexico	1	Italy	1
Ecuador	1	Croatia	0

	P	W	D	L	F	A	Pts
Mexico	3	2	1	0	4	2	7
Italy	3	1	1	1	4	3	4
Croatia	3	1	0	2	2	3	3
Ecuador	3	1	0	2	2	4	3

GROUP H

Japan	2	Belgium	2
Russia	2	Tunisia	0
Japan	1	Russia	0
Tunisia	1	Belgium	1
Japan	2	Tunisia	0
Belgium	3	Russia	2

	P	W	D	L	F	A	Pts
Japan	3	2	1	0	5	2	7
Belgium	3	1	2	0	6	5	5
Russia	3	1	0	2	4	4	3
Tunisia	3	0	1	2	1	5	1

SECOND ROUND

Germany	1	Paraguay	0
England	3	Denmark	0
Senegal	1 [2]	Sweden	1 *
Spain	1 (3)	Rep.Ireland	1 (2)*
United States	2	Mexico	0
Brazil	2	Belgium	0
Turkey	1	Japan	0
South Korea	2	Italy	1 *

* After extra time (pens) [golden goal]

QUARTER-FINALS

Brazil	2	England	1
Germany	1	United States	0
South Korea	0 (5)	Spain	0 (4)*
Turkey	0 [1]	Senegal	0 *

* After extra time (pens) [golden goal]

SEMI-FINALS

Germany	1	South Korea	0
Brazil	1	Turkey	0

THIRD-PLACE MATCH

Turkey	3	South Korea	2

FINAL – June 30: International, Yokohama

Brazil 2 (Ronaldo 68, 79)
Germany 0
HT: 0-0. **Att:** 69,029. **Ref:** Collina (Italy).
Brazil: Marcos, Cafu, Lucio, Roque Junior, Edmilson, Roberto Carlos, Gilberto Silva, Kleberson, Ronaldinho (Juninho 85), Ronaldo (Denilson 90), Rivaldo.
Germany: Kahn, Linke, Ramelow, Metzelder, Bode (Ziege 84), Schneider, Frings, Hamann, Jeremies (Asamoah 78), Neuville, Klose (Bierhoff 74).
Top scorer: 8 Ronaldo (Brazil)

GERMANY 2006

Italy won its fourth World Cup with a penalty shoot-out defeat of France after the teams had drawn 1–1 after 120 minutes in Berlin. The match will remain in the memory more for French captain Zinedine Zidane's red card after his head-butt on his marker than any great soccer played or Fabio Grosso's winning kick. Germany were excellent hosts, not only in terms of organisation, but also on the pitch. Coach Jürgen Klinsmann took his team to third place after derailing the Argentina express in the quarter-finals. The South Americans had played the best soccer in the tournament, highlighted by their 6–0 crushing of Serbia & Montenegro, especially Esteban Cambiasso's goal which involved nine players, 20 passes and 55 touches. England were unimpressive in reaching the quarter-finals, but the injury bug hit hard – Rio Ferdinand, David Beckham and Michael Owen were effectively out of the tournament – even before Wayne Rooney saw red against Portugal and the penalty shoot-out had, for them, its inevitable outcome.

GROUP A

Germany	4	Costa Rica	2
Ecuador	2	Poland	0
Germany	1	Poland	0
Ecuador	3	Costa Rica	0
Germany	3	Ecuador	0
Poland	2	Costa Rica	1

	P	W	D	L	F	A	Pts
Germany	3	3	0	0	8	2	9
Ecuador	3	2	0	1	5	3	6
Poland	3	1	0	2	2	4	3
Costa Rica	3	0	0	3	3	9	0

GROUP B

England	1	Paraguay	0
Trinidad & Tobago	0	Sweden	0
England	2	Trinidad & Tobago	0
Sweden	1	Paraguay	0
Sweden	2	England	2
Paraguay	2	Trinidad & Tobago	0

	P	W	D	L	F	A	Pts
England	3	2	1	0	5	2	7
Sweden	3	1	2	0	3	2	5
Paraguay	3	1	0	2	2	2	3
Trinidad & Tobago	3	0	1	2	0	4	1

GROUP C

Argentina	2	Ivory Coast	1
Serbia & Montenegro	0	Holland	1
Argentina	6	Serbia & Montenegro	0
Holland	2	Ivory Coast	1
Holland	0	Argentina	0
Ivory Coast	3	Serbia & Montenegro	2

	P	W	D	L	F	A	Pts
Argentina	3	2	1	0	8	1	7
Holland	3	2	1	0	3	1	7
Ivory Coast	3	1	0	2	5	6	3
Serbia & Montenegro	3	0	0	3	2	10	0

GROUP D

Mexico	3	Iran	1
Portugal	1	Angola	0
Mexico	0	Angola	0
Portugal	2	Iran	0
Portugal	2	Mexico	1
Iran	1	Angola	1

	P	W	D	L	F	A	Pts
Portugal	3	3	0	0	5	1	9
Mexico	3	1	1	1	4	3	4
Angola	3	0	2	1	1	2	2
Iran	3	0	1	2	2	6	1

GROUP E

Czech Republic	3	USA	0
Italy	2	Ghana	0
Ghana	2	Czech Republic	0
Italy	1	USA	1
Italy	2	Czech Republic	0
Ghana	2	USA	1

	P	W	D	L	F	A	Pts
Italy	3	2	1	0	5	1	7
Ghana	3	2	0	1	4	3	6
Czech Republic	3	1	0	2	3	4	3
USA	3	0	1	2	2	6	1

GROUP F

Australia	3	Japan	1
Brazil	1	Croatia	0
Croatia	0	Japan	0
Brazil	2	Australia	0
Brazil	4	Japan	1
Croatia	2	Australia	2

	P	W	D	L	F	A	Pts
Brazil	3	3	0	0	7	1	9
Australia	3	1	1	1	5	5	4
Croatia	3	0	2	1	2	3	2
Japan	3	0	1	2	2	7	1

GROUP G

South Korea	2	Togo	1
France	0	Switzerland	0
France	1	South Korea	1
Switzerland	2	Togo	0
France	2	Togo	0
Switzerland	2	South Korea	0

	P	W	D	L	F	A	Pts
Switzerland	3	2	1	0	4	0	7
France	3	1	2	0	3	1	5
South Korea	3	1	1	1	3	4	4
Togo	3	0	0	3	1	6	0

GROUP H

Spain	4	Ukraine	0
Tunisia	2	Saudi Arabia	2
Ukraine	4	Saudi Arabia	0
Spain	3	Tunisia	1
Spain	1	Saudi Arabia	0
Ukraine	1	Tunisia	0

	P	W	D	L	F	A	Pts
Spain	3	3	0	0	8	1	9
Ukraine	3	2	0	1	5	4	6
Tunisia	3	0	1	2	3	6	1
Saudi Arabia	3	0	1	2	2	7	1

SECOND ROUND

Germany	2	Sweden	0
Argentina	2	Mexico	1*
Italy	1	Australia	0
Ukraine	0 (3)	Switzerland	0 (0)*
England	1	Ecuador	0
Portugal	1	Netherlands	0
Brazil	3	Ghana	0
France	3	Spain	1

* After extra time (pens)

QUARTER-FINALS

Germany	1 (4)	Argentina	1(2)*
Italy	3	Ukraine	0
Portugal	0 (3)	England	0 (1)*
France	1	Brazil	0

* After extra time (pens)

SEMI-FINALS

Italy	2	Germany	0*
France	1	Portugal	0

* After extra time

THIRD-PLACE MATCH

Germany	3	Portugal	1

FINAL – July 9: Olympiastadion, Berlin

Italy 1 (5) (Materazzi 19)
France 1 (3) (Zidane 7 (pen))*
HT: 1-1. **Att:** 69,000. **Ref:** Elizondo (Argentina)
Italy: Buffon, Zambrotta, Cannavaro, Materazzi, Grosso, Gattuso, Pirlo, Camoranesi (Del Piero 86), Perrotta (De Rossi 61), Totti (Iaquinta 61), Toni.
France: Barthez, Sagnol, Thuram, Gallas, Abidal, Vieira (Diarra 56), Makélélé, Ribéry (Trezeguet 100), Zidane, Malouda, Henry (Wiltord 107). **Sent off:** Zidane.
Top scorer: 5 Klose (Germany)

* After extra time (pens)

Right: Italy captain Fabio Cannavaro holds aloft the 2006 World Cup. This was Italy's fourth World Cup win.

The publishers would like to thank the following sources for their kind permission to reproduce the pictures in this book. The page numbers for each of the photographs are listed below, giving the page on which they appear in the book and any location indicator (C-centre, T-top, B-bottom, L-left, R-right).

Getty Images: /AFP: 23TR; /Gallo Images: 23BR; /Alexander Joe/AFP: 22BR; /Richard Rad/Latin Content: 36, 37

Press Association Images: /AP: 62, 69T; /Barry Aldworth/Sports Inc: 108; /Hassan Ammar/AP: 17; /Matthew Ashton/Empics Sport: 103B; /Olivier Asselin/AP: 32; /Frank Augstein/AP: 57B; /David Azia/AP: 4; /Gavin Barker/Sports Inc: 27, 52, 72, 90, 111; /Luigi Bennett/Sports Inc: 26; /Fabian Bimmer/AP: 77B; /Rebecca Blackwell/AP: 94; /Abdeljalil Bounhar/AP: 81T; /Luca Bruno/AP: 97T; /Lynne Cameron/PA Archive: 74, 75B; /Barry Coombs/Empics Sport: 76, 77T, 78, 82, 93T, 100, 101B; /Claudio Cruz/AP: 45B; /Andres Cuenca/AP: 47T; /David Davies/PA Wire: 24TL; /Adam Davy/Empics Sport: 16, 21, 22TL, 23TL, 42, 43T, 56, 60, 73T, 79T, 91T, 98, 99T, 101T; /Sean Dempsey/PA Archive: 58, 59T; /Mike Egerton/Empics Sport: 34, 68, 97B, 114, 127; /Empics Sport: 33, 54, 55T, 55B, 96, 118; /Dominic Favre/AP: 109; /Esteban Felix/AP: 102; /Nigel French/Empics Sport: 105T, 105B; /Clive Gee/PA Archive: 53T, 53B; /Petros Giannakouris/AP: 57; /Joe Giddens/Empics Sport: 43B, 81B, 89T, 89B; /Nicolas Gouhier/ABACA: 49B; /Themba Hadebe/AP: 24-25; /Nam Y Huh/AP: 9; /Mark Humphrey/AP: 10; /Srdjan Ilic/AP: 71B; /Matthew Impey/Empics Sport: 73B; /Itsuo Inouye/AP: 79B; /Silvia Izquierdo/AP: 104; /Hasan Jamali/AP: 86; /Georgios Kefalas/AP: 83T; /Peter Kneffel/DPA: 67T; /Lee Jin-Man/AP: 92, 93B; /Fernando Llano/AP: 46; /Daniel Luna/AP: 47B; /Sydney Mahlangu/Sports Inc: 23BL, 87B; /Tony Marshall/Empics Sport: 13, 44, 45T, 64, 65B, 71T, 84, 103T; /Steeve McMay/ABACA: 48; /Martin Meissner/AP: 31, 99B, 115; /Sabelo Mngoma/Sports Inc: 22BL; /Peter Morrison/AP: 69B; /Stuart Morton/ABACA: 63T; /Andre Penner/AP: 91B; /Gabriel Piko/PikoPress: 110; /Daniel Piris/AP: 85T, 85B; /Natacha Pisarenko/AP: 51B; /Stephen Pond/Empics Sport: 51T, 63B, 66; /Nick Potts: 83B; /Dean Purcell/AP: 87T; /Guillaume Ramon/ABACA: 49T; /Dusan Ranic/AP: 95T; /Martin Rickett/PA Archive: 59B; /Joerg Sarbach/AP: 112; /Ross Setford/AP: 30, 35; /Shajor/PikoPress: 50; /Neal Simpson/Empics Sport: 88; /Jon Super/AP: 67B; /J-Paul Thomas/Panoramic: 95B; /Paul Thomas/AP: 11, 19; /Erik Vandenbuch/ABACA: 61T, 61B; /Marco Vasini/AP: 65T; /Claudio Villa/Grazia Neri: 113; /Darko Vojinovic/AP: 70; /John Walton/Empics Sport: 75T, 80; /Nick Wass/AP: 6; /Bernd Weissbrod/DPA: 22TR; /Ryan Wilkisky/Sports Inc: 24BL

Every effort has been made to acknowledge correctly and contact the source and/or copyright holder of each picture and any unintentional errors or omissions that will be corrected in future editions of this book.